THE
COMPLETE
KODAK
BOOK OF
PHOTOGRAPHY

This volume was abridged by Thomas Dickey and Don Earnest from the KODAK Library of Creative Photography, a series of books created and designed by Mitchell Beazley International in association with Kodak and Time-Life Books.

Revised and updated by Jonathan Vince

Commissioning Editor Sarah Polden
Art Editor John Grain

Staff for the KODAK Library of Creative Photography

Mitchell Beazley International

Editor-in-Chief
Jack Tresidder

Series Editors
John Roberts, Robert Saxton

Art Editors
Mel Petersen, Mike Brown

Editors
Ian Chilvers, Louise Earwaker, Lucy Lidell, Joss Pearson, Richard Platt, Carolyn Ryden

Designers
Robert Lamb, Marnie Searchwell, Michelle Stamp, Lisa Tai, Ruth Prentice

Assistant Designers
Stewart Moore, Susan Rentoul

Picture Researchers
Brigitte Arora, Jackum Brown, Veneta Bullen, Nicky Hughes, Beverly Tunbridge

Editorial Assistant
Margaret Little

Production
Peter Phillips, Jean Rigby, Androulla Pavlou

Chief Consulting Photographer
Michael Freeman

Consulting Photographers
Michael Busselle, Tony Duffy, Donald Honeyman, Steve Powell, Tim Stephens

Coordinating Editors for Kodak
John Fish, Ken Lassiter, Paul Mulroney, Ken Oberg, Jackie Salitan

Consulting Editor for Time-Life Books
Thomas Dickey

Published by Lowe & B. Hould Publishers, an imprint of Borders, Inc., by arrangement with Random House Value Publishing, Inc.
All rights reserved.

Lowe & B. Hould is a trademark of Borders Properties, Inc.
311 Maynard, Ann Arbor, MI 48104

ISBN 0-681-22005-8

10, 9, 8, 7, 6, 5, 4, 3, 2, 1

Produced by Mandarin Offset
Printed and bound in China

Kodak is a trade mark of Kodak Limited and its related companies

ABOUT THIS BOOK

The best photographs are simple. They convey a message directly and vividly, whether it be the joy of a family reunion or the splendor of a canyon lit by the evening sky. This same simplicity often applies to the way photographs are taken, especially now that modern cameras and film have made dealing with exposure and other technical problems much easier – freeing the photographer's eye and imagination. The aim of this book is to show that everyone, from novices to experienced enthusiasts, can transform their photography with simple techniques and clear creative principles.

This book thoroughly explores the equipment, techniques and subjects available to you, whatever your interest and level of experience. Throughout, the focus is on taking pictures with a 35mm camera, the tool favored by dedicated amateurs as well as professionals for its versatility and convenience.

The first part of the book, "What Makes A Good Picture," begins by showing you basic compositional principles; understanding them will develop your most important piece of equipment – your eye. You will then learn how to handle a camera, get the right exposure and use color imaginatively.

The second part of the book, "Pictures of Ourselves," is devoted to the favorite subject of most photographers – people – with advice on capturing the likenesses and activities of family and friends, taking formal and candid portraits and photographing nudes.

In "The World Around Us," which explores the popular subjects of travel and nature, you will learn about the tools and techniques for recording landscapes, wildlife and the most pleasurable moments of a trip.

The fourth and final part of the book, "Extending Your Range," covers the techniques you need to explore advanced image-making and the special subjects that interest you. You will become familiar with how to capture action, create special effects, handle special lighting conditions and use basic studio techniques. A section on the home darkroom gives step-by-step instructions on developing and printing your own pictures. And the book concludes by showing you how to present your prints and slides in the most interesting fashion.

In short, you will find – on pages filled with inspiring and informative images – all the practical advice you need to take exciting, memorable pictures of your own.

CONTENTS

WHAT MAKES A GOOD PICTURE?

Page 16

32 YOU, THE PHOTOGRAPHER
34 Seeing pictures
36 Identifying the subject
38 Studied images, fleeting moments
40 A moment's thought
42 Choosing the best viewpoint
44 Deciding the format
46 The main point of interest
48 Harmony and balance
50 Form and the image
52 Pattern
54 The strength of line
56 Surface texture

58 YOU AND YOUR CAMERA
60 Light, lens and film
62 The camera you use
64 What to do first
66 Focusing the image
68 The shutter
70 The aperture
72 How lenses control the image
74 The size we see
76 Widening the view
78 Concentrating the view
80 Recording everything sharply
82 Isolating what is important
84 The right film
86 Choosing black-and-white film
88 Choosing color film
90 Slide film
92 Print film

94 MAKE LIGHT WORK FOR YOU
96 Controlling light
98 Measuring light
100 Manual and automatic/1
102 Manual and automatic/2
104 The exposure you want
106 Into the light
108 Raking light
110 Sunlight controlled
112 Handling limited light
114 Using flash
116 Using simple filters

118 USING COLOR CREATIVELY
120 The richness of color
122 The dominant color
124 Limited color
126 Color harmony
128 Dramatic color
130 Abstract color
132 Saturated color
134 Muted color
136 The balance of color/1
138 The balance of color/2

PICTURES OF OURSELVES

Page 140

156 PEOPLE AT THEIR BEST
158 Expressing personality
160 Relaxing the subject
162 At work and play
164 The right lens
166 The ideal light
168 Backlight and silhouettes
170 Modifying the light
172 Using flash
174 Toddlers
176 Brothers, sisters and friends
178 Parent and child
180 Parents and grandparents
182 Wedding day/1
184 Wedding day/2
186 The snapshot style
188 Dealing with strangers
190 Faces in the crowd

192 THE ART OF PORTRAITS
194 Choosing a pose
196 Full-face or profile?
198 Full-length portraits
200 Closing in
202 Candid portraits
204 Faces and features
206 The outdoor portrait
208 Natural light indoors
210 Lighting faces/1
212 Lighting faces/2
214 Group portraits
216 Self-portraits

218 PHOTOGRAPHING THE NUDE
220 The simple approach
222 Human geometry
224 Form and figure
226 Texture and the body
228 The minimal approach
230 Nudes in landscapes
232 The studio nude

THE WORLD AROUND US

Page 234

250 THE TRAVELING CAMERA
252 What to take
254 Judging a location
256 Classic sites
258 Everyday living
260 The original approach
262 Developing a theme
264 The special event
266 Exotic glimpses
268 The picture essay/1
270 The picture essay/2

272 THE NATURAL LANDSCAPE
274 The spirit of the place
276 Viewpoint and scope
278 Viewpoint and depth
280 The marks of man
282 Exploiting drama
284 Patterns in nature
286 Trees and forests
288 Sea and shore
290 Mountain landscapes
292 Natural forces
294 Sky and wind

296 ANIMALS AND PLANTS
298 Finding animals
300 Dress and equipment
302 Telephoto lenses
304 Birds in flight
306 Getting closer
308 Using vehicles
310 Wildlife with flash
312 Animals in town and garden
314 Animals at the zoo
316 Flowers/1
318 Flower/2

EXTENDING YOUR RANGE

Page 320

336 CATCHING THE ACTION
338 The action around us
340 Fast shutter
342 Fast film
344 Prefocusing
346 Panning
348 Blurring movement
350 Track and field
352 Winter sports
354 On the water
356 Indoor sports

358 CREATING SPECIAL EFFECTS
360 Unexpected angles
362 Tricks with a slow shutter
364 Tricks with flash
366 Zooming
368 Filters for simple effects/1
370 Filters for simple effects/2
372 Starburst and diffraction filters
374 Photography through screens
376 Multi-image filters
378 Split-field close-up lenses
380 Transposing film
382 Double exposure
384 Projected images
386 Sandwiching

388 SPECIAL CONDITIONS
390 Rain and storm
392 Ice and snow
394 The glare of the sun
396 Twilight and night
398 Flames
400 Tungsten lighting
402 Other artificial light
404 Stage lighting
406 Zooming challenges
408 Underwater photography

410 STUDIO TECHNIQUES
412 One-lamp lighting
414 Multiple light sources
416 Arranging the lighting/1
418 Arranging the lighting/2
420 Composing the still-life
422 The calculated illusion

424 THE HOME DARKROOM
426 Black-and-white darkroom equipment
428 Developing black-and-white film/1
430 Developing black-and-white film/2
432 Making a contact sheet
434 Black-and-white printing/1
436 Black-and-white printing/2
438 Basic control techniques
440 Color darkroom equipment
442 Processing color negatives/1
444 Processing color negatives/2
446 Making a test print
448 Testing filtration
450 Making a final print
452 Printing from transparencies/1
454 Printing from transparencies/2
456 Printing from transparencies/3

458 PRESENTING YOUR PICTURES
460 Editing photographs
462 Showing slides
464 Sequencing a slide show
466 Showing prints
468 Glossary
473 Index
477 Picture credits

WHAT MAKES A GOOD PICTURE?

Our response to a picture is guided by the subject matter and by personal taste. But apart from that, two things are fundamentally important in any picture: composition and light. For the picture opposite, the photographer used the massive tree to touchingly frame the child's small figure. Along with this compositional device, the soft light and colors contribute strongly to the picture's mood.

The pictures in the following portfolio exemplify some of the important elements of composition: balance and asymmetry, shape and form, pattern and texture. They are at the core of creative photography, as is light, which is not only necessary to form a photographic image, but is a compositional tool in its own right. To create photographs that have calculated effects, you must know how to vary the quality and direction of light as well as its quantity. Similarly, you can use color to create delight, impact, variety – and you can even make color itself the subject of a picture.

This first part of the book shows you how you can turn these elements into practical ways of improving your pictures. Any good photographer is, of course, familiar with his equipment, and one section will help familiarize you with cameras and film. But good photographers also recognize that much of their work must be done before the shutter is pressed. Ultimately, the ability to produce strong images unerringly, rather than by chance, depends on looking long and hard at your subject, analyzing what you see, and planning what to do.

An expert eye captured this image of a little girl playing in a park. The picture's charm stems largely from the photographer's decision to fill most of the frame with the tree's autumn colors, which are accentuated by diffuse light.

Perfect balance *gives this architectural view a sense of calm elegance. The photographer carefully exploited the symmetry of the paired trees, branched lamp and pilasters behind.*

Deliberate asymmetry here establishes an unsettled mood. The lonely figure, framed so that he crosses the very top of the picture, emphasizes the emptiness of a concrete landscape.

Rainy weather, *often thought unsuitable for photography,
creates some of the most interesting photographic opportunities.
Amateur Luis Huesco took advantage of it when he was on a tour
of a Spanish museum. Through a half-open door, he noticed the
chance presented by two children playing alone in a drenched
courtyard. In spite of their rushing figures, the scene seems
charged with an eerie stillness, an effect created by the weather's
gray mood in the symmetrical setting.*

The inspired pattern of this unusual image came from the photographer's simple realization that a plaything such as a badminton shuttlecock can cast fascinating shadows when placed in front of a strong light source. By mating a pair of shuttlecocks in the light of a slide projector, the delicate ribbed wings of a shadow-insect were created.

The beauty of a woman,
her smile, and her patterned
sweater are brought out by
a setting that reveals the
photographer's eye for the
way colors work together.
The vivid red background
and the frame of dark bricks
complement perfectly the
subtle hues of the sweater.

Pale balloons *float against a somber background of shadowed architecture in a composition that deliberately restricts color to a small area of the frame. The surprising impact of the picture demonstrates the power of color to sway us with the lightest touch.*

Beach umbrellas, *abandoned during a rain shower, sweep in a delicate green arc across the whole picture. The blending and softening of hues on a misty day such as this often creates marvelous opportunities for color photographs.*

Windblown barley has been blurred here by the choice of a shutter speed too slow to stop the tips of the stalks waving. By this means the photographer has subtly muted the overall color to pale green.

The sparkle of a smile
and the bright red of a sun
hat in the picture above
lend the simplest of portraits
an infectious gaiety. The
photographer moved in close
to frame the girl against the
plain white wall and intensify
the impact of the peaked cap
above her glowing face.

The yellow rain hat pulled
over the child's face makes a
telling portrait that needed
only an open response to the
sudden opportunity. Many
photographers would have
waited, or asked the boy to
lift the hat up again for a
clear view, missing the
drama of the invisible face.

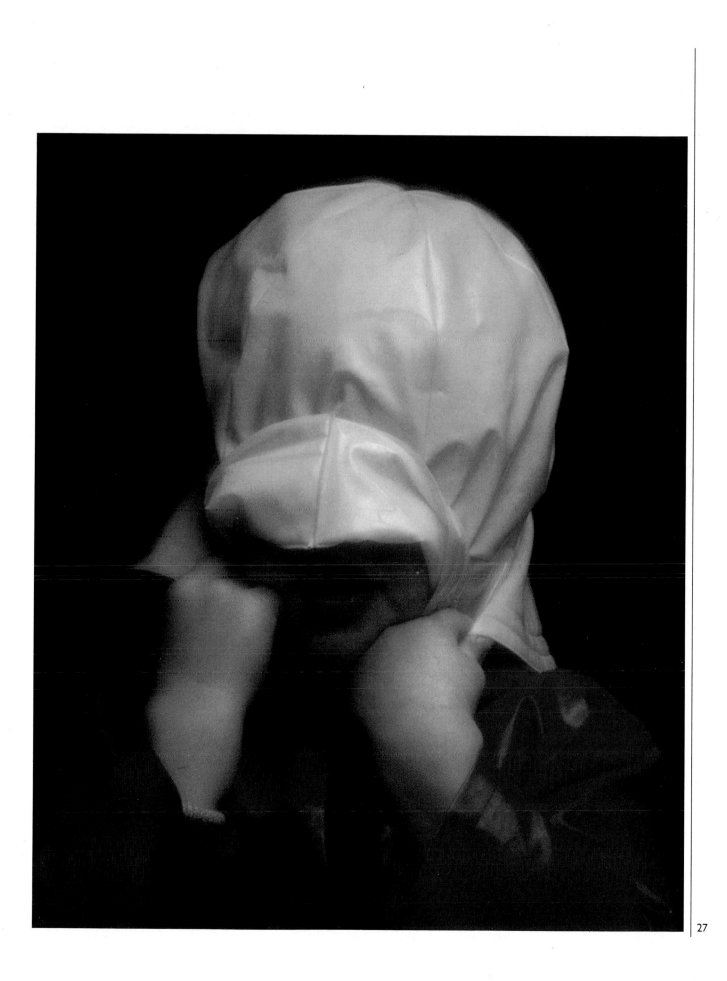

A fast shutter *(left)*
crisply suspends a boy in
midair as he heads a soccer
ball. By also deliberately
underexposing the backlit
subject, the photographer
silhouetted him against the
soft, unfocused background.

A slow shutter *(above)*
helped to convey a child's
imagined speed as he plays
Superman. The long exposure
allowed the camera to follow
the boy as he crossed the
frame, creating streaks of
moving color in the
background. This also blurred
the motion of his legs so that
he seems about to take off.

Blurred water – *achieved by a slow shutter speed – in this somber landscape has smoothed out the one active element of the scene and turned the picture into a hauntingly beautiful still-life. The strange effect was surprisingly easy to create, needing no more than a time exposure of a few seconds.*

30

*A majestic baboon, isolated
by a telephoto lens, displays
the soft colors and strongly
defined patterns of his facial
markings. Like many good
animal shots, this is not an
exotic wildlife picture: the
photographer spotted the
baboon in the shady doorway
of its zoo den, and closed in.*

31

YOU, THE PHOTOGRAPHER

Good photographs come from developing an eye for a picture – not from using banks of powerful studio lights, whirring motor-drives, or two-foot-long telephoto lenses. Success requires no more than the ability to make the essential creative leap from what you see to what will work as a photographic image. The secret of doing this is to train the eye to see images that will give pleasure when they are taken out of the complex, confused, and constantly shifting world and made into photographs isolated by their frames.

Experienced photographers become adept at identifying interesting images largely because they spend a great deal of time looking through the viewfinders of their cameras. Anyone can learn to see pictures in the same way. Look through the viewfinder frequently, even when you do not intend to take a picture. Concentrate on what you can actually see in the frame and how the shapes or colors there work together. You can practice this way of seeing even when you do not have a camera with you – remember the old artist's trick of holding the hands up as a frame? This creative and imaginative process is at the heart of photography, and the pictures on the following pages emphasize how much effective images depend on vision itself.

The viewfinder is your photographic link with the world in front of the camera. Here, the edges of its frame isolate four silhouetted figures from the bustle of a city park. The picture is compelling because the photographer used the camera's special eye to select the right image at the right moment.

Seeing pictures

Distant details, such as the woman walking her dog, may attract the eye, but are not clearly visible. However, with a telephoto lens, the camera can close in on such images.

To begin seeing as the camera sees, you need to recognize its basic powers – and limitations. First, consider the similarities between the camera and the eye. Both use a lens to focus an image on a surface that is sensitive to light. And a camera has ways of controlling the intensity of the incoming light, much as the pupil of the eye does. But, while these parallels are interesting, the differences are actually more relevant when you try to take pictures. In particular, the eye has vastly greater flexibility, working automatically in a way that the most advanced electronic camera cannot emulate.

Because you have two eyes, your brain receives two views of any subject from slightly different angles. Fused together into a single image, they form a picture that gives you a greater sense of depth than any photograph could provide. Moreover, the camera takes in the whole scene with uncritical interest, whereas your eyes concentrate on the parts of the scene you find most interesting.

The focus of the eye can change so swiftly from near to far objects that all appear equally in focus.

A boy playing may move too fast for the eye to capture his actions. But the camera can freeze every detail – even the ball in mid-air.

The eye
The remarkable versatility of human vision stems from the close link between the eye and the brain. Without our being consciously aware of the process, the brain controls the eye as it rapidly scans a scene to build up a complete picture, focusing on various details and adjusting to differing light levels. At the same time, the brain interprets the information received, making sense, for example, of the changes in scale between objects as they appear to diminish in size with distance. Vision extends through a full 160, compared with the 45 view of a normal camera lens.

Images from the real world
Photographs may look like
the real world – but do not
duplicate the eye's view,
here represented by a hand-
tinted, retouched image.
This scene in a park around ·
a mansion includes several
photographic subjects, some
of which are reproduced in
the insets. Each inset picture
captures an image different
from one the eye would see.

The camera, however, can focus only a part of the scene in one picture. The eye is also a great deal more flexible in handling extreme contrasts in the light level. Within the same scene, we can distinguish details of objects in deep shadow and in bright sunlight in a way that is denied to the camera.

On the other hand, the camera has certain powers that are beyond those of the eye. By framing a small part of the world and thus engaging our attention, a photograph can make us see things that might otherwise go unnoticed. And the camera's ability to freeze motion can reveal details of moving objects not always visible to the naked eye.

Perhaps the most essential of all these things to remember is that your eye can notice instantaneously what interests you in a scene and ignore the rest, shifting attention constantly from the whole to the smallest detail in a changing stream. The camera, by contrast, fixes the whole scene in the viewfinder at the moment you press the shutter. You must provide the discrimination by so directing the camera that worthwhile images are selected.

*The man is the subject
for an impromptu portrait.
Notice how the camera has
framed him and isolated him
from his surroundings. The
lens's shallow focus shows
the background as a blur,
removing any distraction.*

The camera
The camera's relative lack of flexibility means that
you must operate it carefully to record effective
images. First, focus must be adjusted for the subject
to appear sharp. The amount of light allowed to fall
on the film must also be just right – and even then
the contrast between light and dark areas in a scene
may be too great for detail to show in both. On the
other hand, the camera records an image fixed in time,
allowing us to keep a record of visual experiences
that we want to remember. Photographs can also show
details of movement the eye could never catch.

Identifying the subject

The first creative step in taking a photograph is to choose the subject. This may seem obvious, but any one situation usually offers a wide range of choices. As a general rule, you should look for a subject that will make a single strong point. The more elements there are in the scene, the more important it is to have a clear idea about what you want the picture to show at the moment you press the shutter. If there are too many details in the viewfinder that do not support the main point, the picture will tend to look untidy – a random snap rather than an effective photograph. As we have just seen, the camera, unlike the eye, is not capable of concentrating on what is interesting and ignoring the rest. Everything in the viewfinder tends to have equal prominence unless the photographer organizes the scene and selects the image to bring out a particular part or aspect of it.

With an inherently disorganized scene – a crowded beach, for example – you need a good deal of skill to produce a broad view that does not look untidy, although the rich variety seen in a panoramic shot may have its own interest. The solution may be to find a viewpoint that allows you to simplify the picture down to a few elements. The photographs on these two pages illustrate three ways of simplifying the picture – moving in on a subject, pointing the camera downward to cut out extraneous background detail, and using a vertical format to concentrate on a single figure.

A conventional panorama of the beach records the overall scene without directing your attention to any feature in particular. The subject is full of other interesting photographic possibilities.

The solitary bather (right) is the subject rather than the confusion of surf. Attention is drawn to her by the footprints the photographer has carefully lined up in the viewfinder before taking the picture.

A downward shot from a hotel balcony produces a forceful picture because the photographer chose as a subject the strong graphic pattern of umbrellas and sunbathers.

A close–up of a little girl's delight as a wave leaves her stranded excludes distracting detail and frames her as the entire subject of the picture within a plain blue background.

Studied images, fleeting moments

Sometimes the world around us moves so fast that we experience moments of action, excitement, or laughter almost as a passing blur. The camera's ability to freeze these moments and record them on film is one of photography's most remarkable attributes and many of the pictures that give greatest pleasure are those that exploit it. But in other photographs what impresses is the sense of absolute stillness and order. This is often the result of the photographer's having had time to think hard about a stationary scene and perhaps rearrange it to make an image that is thoroughly balanced, as in the picture of a hotel balcony on this page.

There are thus two contrasting approaches to taking pictures. On the one hand, an alert photographer can capture those high points and instants in time that may never return – a child's first faltering steps, or a spontaneous burst of laughter in a game. The only way to be sure of catching these fleeting events consistently is to learn to anticipate

them. This means having the camera ready, out of its case, with the film wound on and the controls set to the approximate light conditions and focusing distance. From then on, it is a matter of quick reactions, accurate timing – and a little luck – to be able to capture pictures with the immediacy of the two images at the top of the page opposite.

The other, more considered, approach requires patience together with something of the artist's eye for composition. With time and care, even the simplest objects can be arranged to make an attractive picture and one that perhaps is alive in a different way – because it is charged with atmosphere. The key to successful pictures of this kind is often the lighting, which may be precisely controlled by the photographer. Even natural light can be controlled, if only by standing at a well-judged angle to the subject you are photographing or by waiting for the transformations in a landscape that occur as the sun moves or is covered by clouds.

The warmth and peace of a holiday balcony is evoked precisely in an image that seems as casual as the towel draped on the chair. In fact the photographer carefully studied the angle of the chair, adjusted the louvered doors as a frame, and waited until the sun lit the green slats on one side, leaving the others dark.

Landscapes like the one at right may last only seconds as sunlight bursts through storm clouds. The photographer had forseen the dramatic instant of brilliant contrast.

A gust of wind flips off the cyclist's hat –
but the photographer was ready to catch
the instant of surprise and amusement. He
had preset the camera controls as the
cyclist approached a corner.

Spontaneity and contrivance mix in this
picture by a photographer who gave the
boy the bubble gum so that he would relax
for the camera – and then snapped off a
remarkably natural and relaxed portrait.

A moment's thought

Many first-time camera users set about taking pictures assuming that everything will fall automatically into place. They aim the lens directly toward the subject, lining up the most important features with the center of the viewfinder as though the camera were a kind of rifle and the subject a target. This approach will certainly record the subject on film, but is unlikely to produce an appealing image. You will achieve better results by thinking for a few seconds and allowing yourself time to study the scene in the viewfinder carefully. Are there distracting elements in the frame that would be better excluded by changing the camera position? Is a vertical format – used for the shot here of the reflected building – more suited to the subject than a horizontal one? Are there patterns – as in the rodeo picture – that can be used to give the picture a bold visual structure? With practice, this self-questioning process becomes automatic, a rapid sequence of mental trial and error. But for the beginner – and even for the expert – a conscious pause for thought can make all the difference between an ordinary snapshot and a picture with real impact.

A few simple ideas can point the way. First, placing the main subject slightly off-center in the frame can create a more balanced and visually satisfying effect than composing directly around the picture's center. The picture of the old woman opposite is a fine example. Pay particular attention to any lines in the scene – they can be used to direct the attention of a viewer around the picture. Strong lines can also affect the mood you want to achieve – diagonals suggest direction and even movement, and are useful for leading the eye into and out of the picture. These are only a few of the elements of composition that you should take into account in making a picture something more than a visual jumble – and many more will become apparent as you begin to develop visual awareness.

Closing in on this row of cowgirls and using a vertical format eliminates the confused background of a rodeo scene – a simple yet often effective compositional technique. The real subject is the central woman, framed by her two similarly dressed companions. Though they are abruptly cropped by the picture's edge, they are still important in providing pattern and balancing the whole image.

Alone in a wheatfield, the child dominates the landscape although occupying only a small part of the picture area. The photographer moved back and up the hill to keep horizon and sky out of the shot and make the wheatfield into a single, simple background of warm color.

Reflections can produce intriguing images. Here, amateur Herb Gustafson used observation and forethought to frame the clock tower of the old Federal Courthouse at St Paul, Minnesota, as a reflected vertical in the glass wall of a modern building opposite.

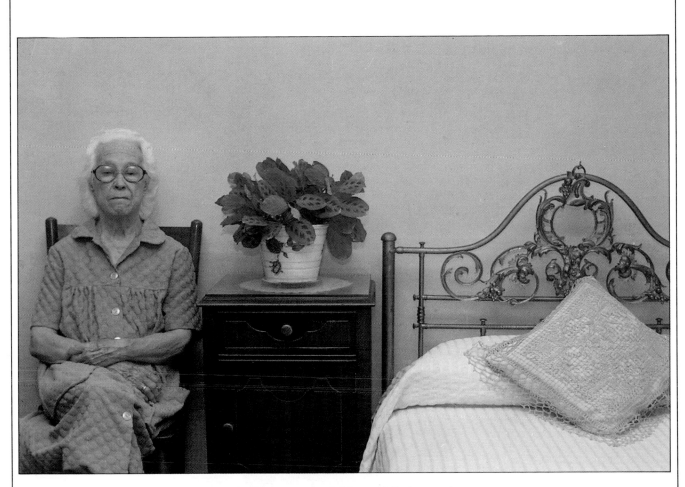

A remarkable portrait of old age, *full of atmosphere,*
relies for its impact on an imaginative composition in which the
subject appears at the very edge of the frame. Center stage is
occupied by an unassuming potted plant. The visual balance
between the old woman and the bed, with its quilt similar in color
to her clothing, helps convey the sense of silence and stillness.

Choosing the best viewpoint

Changing the viewpoint is a photographer's most important means of controlling the way the picture will look. Sometimes moving the camera only slightly can transform the whole composition. Indeed, one of the easiest ways to improve your pictures is to make a habit of moving around the subject to find the best camera position whenever you spot something you wish to photograph.

Seen from a level camera position, most scenes consist of a foreground, a middle distance and a background. The relative positions of objects on these planes can be altered dramatically by shifting viewpoint. Imagine a scene with a field in the foreground, a house in the middle distance, and a tree behind it in the background. Simply by moving your camera to the right, you will place the house to the left of the tree. A lower viewpoint might bring flowers in the field into the close foreground; a higher view would reduce the amount of sky in the frame. By moving back, you could make the house appear smaller and perhaps bring extra foreground elements, such as an overhanging branch of a tree, into the photograph.

The photographs below illustrate how very different the same scene can look from various camera angles. Only by exploring all of the possible viewpoints before taking a picture can you hope to arrive at the best one. Of course, any subject may present you with a number of good viewpoints, all of which will produce equally satisfactory images. Then, your choice must depend on the aspects of the scene you find most interesting. An excellent way to learn both the techniques of composition, and the particular approaches to a subject that suit you, is to take a series of photographs from different positions and then compare the results. This might seem to involve a waste of film, but you will very likely gain insights that will save you film in the future.

Four aspects of a single scene
The Acropolis in Athens is one of the world's most photographed landmarks. These photographs demonstrate how moving the position of the camera can radically alter your impressions of the scene. In the first image, the buildings occupy the middle distance as overall shapes against the hills and sky. For the view at far right, the photographer moved in to silhouette the columns. The distant viewpoint below puts the classical monument into the context of a large modern city. Finally, the panoramic photograph, including tiny figures, provides a human scale.

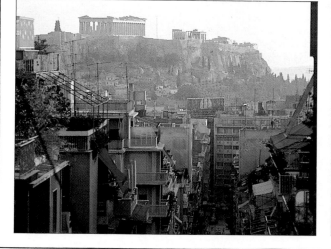
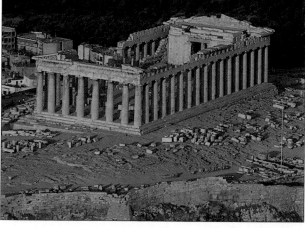

A tennis player throws up a ball to serve. The choice of viewpoint has fully exploited the explosive tension of the sport. When he had posed the subject, the photographer lay on the ground and aimed upward using a wide-angle lens. Thus, the lower half of the server's body appears distorted, emphasizing his leg muscles and long reach.

Deciding the format

Usually one of the major decisions a photographer must make is whether to hold the camera horizontally or vertically. You do not face this choice with cameras that provide a square image. But with a normal 35mm camera, the proportions of the frame are strongly rectangular, and the positioning of this frame is often crucial in terms of both composition and content.

Because holding a camera horizontally is easier than holding it vertically, novices frequently take pictures this way without really considering the alternative. Of course, some subjects naturally suggest a vertical picture – for example, full-length figures, towers or tall buildings. However, even with these subjects there are situations in which you can compose the picture as either a horizontal or an upright image, as demonstrated by the two pictures here of a skyscraper.

Horizontal pictures usually create a more static, peaceful effect than do vertical images, which psychologically suggest vigor – the overcoming of gravity. Sometimes the best images are those that run counter to our expectations. Photographers refer to landscape format to mean a horizontal picture, and portrait format to denote an upright one. Yet a vertically composed landscape may bring interesting foreground or background details into the frame; and a horizontal portrait may be highly effective, as in the example below, in which the off-center placing makes the picture less rigid.

A New York skyscraper, reflected in the mirrored glass of a neighboring building, is intriguingly geometric in the horizontal format above, but gains thrust and impact when viewed vertically in the picture opposite.

The double portrait at left works naturally as an upright composition, the format helping to reinforce the lively upward movement suggested by the pose of the two girls.

A deep-blue door made a perfect background for the man in a blue sweater, and the photographer's first thought was to position him on the axis of the cross-bars in an upright portrait format. However, the effect was too static. By moving slightly to the right and holding the camera horizontally, he achieved a more successful asymmetrical composition.

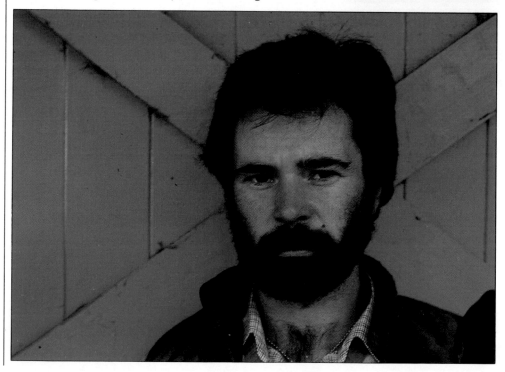

The main point of interest

Whatever the subject, a picture is likely to have greatest impact if there is a main point of interest in the composition. Thus, before you decide how to approach a subject, try to identify the essential focus of attention.

Sometimes the center of interest is easy to spot. For example, the face usually dominates in a portrait, whereas in a landscape a particular tree, hill or stretch of water may provide the key element. When there is no obvious main point, you may have to look harder – or even create one.

Once you have a clear idea of what the main element in the picture should be, start thinking about how you can give prominence to this feature and ensure that other details in the scene do not compete for attention. Three very effective methods – used singly or in combination – will help to achieve this emphasis. First, you can frame the subject in such a way that distracting details are eliminated. In the picture at left below, the photographer excluded the horizon line, which would have marred the effect of the net outlined against the water. Second, you can make use of color or tonal contrasts between the subject and surrounding areas, as in the pictures of the beach sign and the bowler. Third, you can limit the depth of field by selecting a wide aperture and closing in on the main point, so that the subject appears in sharp relief. Both the bowler and the rose at bottom right on the opposite page were picked out in this way.

The strong shapes of both the net and the fisherman required careful framing to limit the picture to these vital elements. The photographer chose a vertical format and aimed the camera downward to eliminate the horizon and obtain a plain background.

The signpost, one small detail in a cluttered beach scene, would lack any impact if photographed from a distance. The photographer spotted the graphic shape and exciting color contrast, and moved in close to isolate the subject from unimportant foreground elements.

At ground level with a 200mm lens, the photographer was able to combine dramatically this English lawn bowler's white target and his curious pose as he sent down another bowl from 30 yards away. The telephoto lens helped to isolate the subject with its narrow angle of view and a shallow depth of field.

1

2

3

Concentrating on the subject
A general view of a dog-rose bush (1) lacks a definite focus of interest. By closing in and framing one main bloom against green leaves (2), the photographer improved the picture. Opening the aperture wider (3) isolated a single in-focus flower.

47

Harmony and balance

The basic principles of composition that underlie most successful photographs are not rules to be followed slavishly. But understanding them will help you to produce balanced and pleasing images.

A key principle is that the main subject should occupy a strong position in the frame. One method of locating such a position is to divide the scene in the viewfinder into thirds, horizontally and vertically, as shown in the diagram at bottom right on the opposite page. The four intersecting points are all areas of strength within the frame, and placing the main subject a third of the way across the frame can work well providing there are other elements to balance the image. In pictures with a single point of interest, the "golden section" is a more useful principle. This classical rule governing aesthetic proportions places the subject slightly closer to the center, thus avoiding imbalance if there is a large area of empty frame. The diagrams at the top of the opposite page illustrate the difference between these two approaches. Both principles have the practical effect of placing the subject off-center, so that an image is not too symmetrical and static. However, if a subject depends on symmetry for effect, as in the image below, the central position may be the best.

Another important way to create effective pictures is to use lines or tones to lead the viewer's eye toward the main subject. Converging lines will draw the eye, as will a gradation of tones, with a dark-toned foreground leading back to progressively lighter tones around the main point of interest. The landscape photograph below at right shows both of these techniques.

Color relationships can be used to great effect in balancing an image. For example, a small area of bright color, placed on one division of thirds, could keep the eye from being drawn too heavily toward a main subject positioned on the other third. Conversely, strong colors or highlights near an edge of the frame can spoil a composition by diverting attention away from the main point.

The stylized symmetry of the facade at right would have been less striking had the photographer not carefully centered the subject. The picture at right shows how a human figure, when placed on two of the strong lines, adds interest and prevents the image from being too static.

Positions in the frame

The four diagrams show how the positioning of the subject will affect the balance of the composition.

1–This diagram shows the eye's view of the scene.

2–With the main point of the picture in the center, the image is dull.

3–A more interesting effect emerges.with the scene divided into thirds by the figure and the house on the intersections.

4–With the main subject standing alone, the best position is on the golden section, dividing the frame into proportions of eight to five.

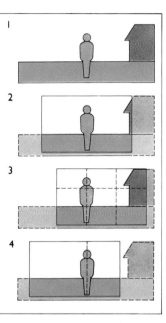

Skeins of wool in perfect visual balance make up a satisfying abstract image. Using a close-up lens, the photographer framed the picture to give more space to the lighter yellow wool, while a loose strand from the weightier blue pulls the elements together.

A tree laden with blossoms commands the horizon. As the diagram below demonstrates, the tree and the yellow field, a supporting subject, both lie on a dividing line of thirds. The slope of the field leads the eye down toward the main point, while the dark foreground draws the viewer into the frame.

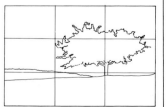

Form and the image

Although shapes alone can make striking images, the information they convey is too limited to show whether an object in a picture has weight, solidity and depth. For this, a viewer needs some indication of form – some variation of light and shade within the outline. Such tonal variations are what give objects the illusion of depth in a photograph.

Light alone governs form, providing the visual clues that convey an object's bumps, hollows, curves or receding surfaces. For example, an orange lit strongly from behind will appear only as a dark, flat disc. But if you soften the light, the shadows on the outer rim will begin to lighten and indicate the orange's curving sides. And if you move the light around so that it falls obliquely on the orange, the gradation of tone from highlights to shadow will reveal the full roundness.

The quality and direction of light best suited to revealing form depends to some extent on the subject. Oblique morning sunlight raking across modern buildings may bring out their angular forms dramatically. But when you want to show more softly rounded curves, as in the picture of weed-covered boulders on the opposite page, the soft light of a cloudy day will give a better impression of form. Bright sun would have thrown a confusing pattern of light and shade over the rocks. For the same reason, moderately diffused light is best for revealing the subtle forms of the face when you want to achieve a balanced effect in portraiture.

Dappled sunlight models the soft, rounded forms of a polar bear and the ledge it stands on. Flatter light would not have separated bear and background so well.

Lustrous grapes, lit obliquely by a low, angled spotlight, have an almost tactile plumpness – an effect created by the play of highlights and shadows.

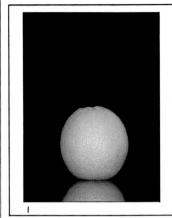 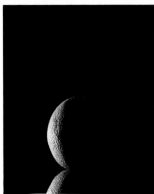 

Light and form
Frontal lighting (1) shows
relatively little of the
orange's form. But harsh
sidelighting (2) also may
disguise form by picking
out only one edge. Softer
light from one side (3),
and the use of a reflector
to direct some light back
to the other side, gives
a truer picture of the
rounded form and the
texture of the orange.

*Sea-washed boulders in
this simple study take on a
sculptural power because
variations of tone and hue,
revealed by diffused light,
convey their rounded weight.*

Pattern

Patterns depend on the repetition of similar shapes, forms, lines or colors. Because such repetitions attract our instinctive attention, they can be a powerful ingredient in photography. And you can easily compose pictures to bring out patterns by identifying repeated elements in a scene and then isolating the part of the view that contains them. In the three pictures here, close framing of much larger subjects has emphasized the patterns they contained and excluded any distracting elements.

Landscapes make excellent subjects for experiments in photographing patterns. The furrows of a plowed field following the contours of the land, or the regularly planted rows of trees, as in the huge olive grove on the opposite page, give visual structure to scenes that might otherwise appear featureless. You can accentuate such patterns when the light from a low sun at right angles to the camera casts shadows that emphasize the repeated shapes of trees or the snaking lines of ridges and hollows in the land. The higher sun of midday tends to fill in the shadows and make a landscape seem flat. For example, in this kind of light the olive trees would have merged more with the parched ground, and their pattern would have been less striking.

The man-made environment is also full of patterns. Standardization of manufactured objects in bold colors and clean shapes creates infinite possibilities for anyone with an alert eye. The umbrellas below were scattered randomly to dry, but the photographer chose a viewpoint that creates order through repetition of shapes, lines and colors.

A lone couple walking in the forest provide a focus for the pattern created by the rows of tall trees lining their way. The photographer centered the path perfectly and kept the camera level so the trees would appear vertical in the picture.

Gaudy umbrellas lie in a jumble that the photographer organized by framing. A small aperture ensured that the entire depth of the subject would be in focus.

Long rows of olive trees
stretch across a Spanish plain,
framed so that their immense
pattern is unrelieved by the
distraction of either sky or
foreground.

The strength of line

Line is often the basis of composition. Look at a scene through half-closed eyes and you will notice that a few strong lines or contours give definition to everything else. At the same time, lines generate a sense of movement into or around a picture space, because we instinctively follow them with our eyes.

Analyzing a random selection of successful photographs will give you an idea of the many ways of exploiting linear effects to support or enhance subjects. Lines can balance an image, drawing the eye toward the main point of interest and linking other elements together, or they can cause discord. The flowing contours of a figure can suggest a supple roundness, as in the picture at the bottom of this page. And at the right time of day, deep shadows in a landscape can create the kind of strong graphic lines seen in the picture of sand dunes below. Although here the flat, solid tones exaggerate the two-dimensional quality of photography, lines can also be a powerful means of creating an illusion of depth. The converging lines of a street or of an avenue of trees receding into the distance are examples of classic linear perspective. The picture of power lines opposite illustrates a more unusual perspective effect: the lines do not meet in the distance, but sweep up sharply out of the frame.

Often the mood of a picture is affected by the sort of lines that dominate. Angles and jagged edges tend to convey a sense of aggression and restless energy, whereas the gentler rhythms of curves, especially those of the human body, can suggest a soft, romantic mood.

Dense shadows create a sinuous ribbon that divides these dunes into abstract shapes. The photographer obtained these strong lines and dramatic tonal contrasts by taking the picture when the sun was low in the sky.

The gentle contour of a nude woman reclining on her side (right) suggests warmth and sensuousness. Broad, diffused light bounced from a large reflector creates a subtle tonal interplay that helps to soften the contour.

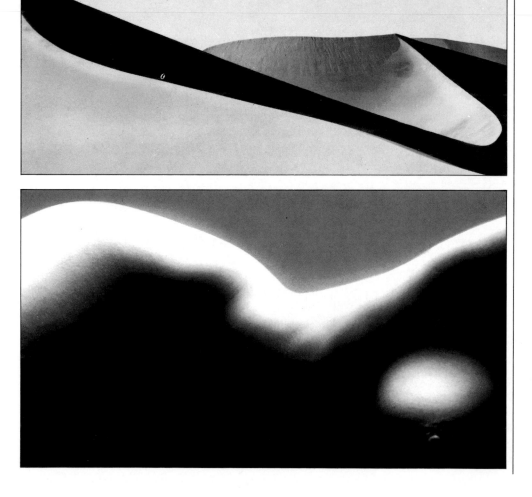

Power cables *spanning a deep valley form a network of fine, intricate lines looping upward out of the frame. The effect of the bright sunlight highlighting the cables makes them stand out boldly against the dark background.*

Surface texture

With the right lighting, you can pick out rugged surfaces in sharp textural relief or reveal a fine texture in surfaces that seem almost completely smooth to the eye. The photographs on these pages show the importance of lighting in recording the different textural characteristics of a range of subjects.

Generally, to bring out texture the light should come from an oblique angle so as to rake the surface of the subject, highlighting each small relief and creating shadows within the indentations. The lower of the two pictures of sculpture at right shows how shadows bring out the relief. A subject with a very delicate texture, such as an eggshell, needs more acutely angled light than does a coarse-textured subject, such as tree bark.

The quality of light is also important. As a rule of thumb, finely textured surfaces need softer, more diffused lighting to bring out their qualities than do rough surfaces in pictures that seek more dramatic effects. The bright highlights and dense shadows cast by strong light will obscure finer details, although a hard light can suit glossy surfaces, such as the painted door at far right.

Oblique light and low relief
Lighting can accentuate or mask a subject's overall texture, as these pictures of an architectural relief sculpture demonstrate.
(1) The soft, diffused light of early morning shows the design as almost flat.
(2) Late in the day, the sun casts a strong, raking sidelight that picks out the relief and the texture of the old, weathered stone.

1

2

A sleeping owl perches in a tree hollow. Soft, low-angled sunlight picks up the pattern of feathers and creates an extraordinary but illusory resemblance between the harsh texture of the ridged bark and the downy softness of the owl.

Rough and smooth, shiny and mat surfaces make an attractive combination in the still-life on the opposite page. Bright, diffused sidelighting brings out the contrasting textures of the crusty loaves of bread, the wooden surfaces and the ceramic pot.

1

2

Oblique light and high relief
The papery seed pods at left have rounded forms that present a higher relief to an oblique light than do the fine sculpted ridges opposite. (1) Soft light shows a delicate tracery of veins in the seed pods, but the picture works mainly as a color pattern. (2) Hard, oblique light shows some texture better, and the shadows bring out the forms of the pods.

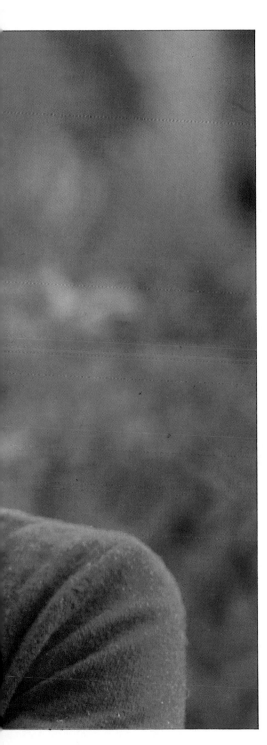

YOU AND YOUR CAMERA

Photography combines two different areas of skill. On the one hand, you need to develop an ability to see creatively, identifying interesting and appealing visual aspects of the world around you. But you also need the ability to translate these photographic ideas into pictures. The camera and film can become efficient servants of your creative impulse – if you learn how to use them.

This is partly a question of mastering essential photographic skills – the principles of camera handling, focusing and exposure that apply to all cameras, however complex or simple. You will handle a camera more confidently if you have a clear understanding of the basic relationship between light, camera and film as explained in the following pages. Try to develop a close familiarity with your own camera also, so that using its controls becomes second nature. The functions and operation of these controls are explained here, but you must study your own camera to see how the principles can be most effectively applied.

Finally, consider your camera in relation to the type of photographs you intend to take. Know the limitations of your equipment and work within them. You will need a camera with a fast shutter to freeze rapid movement, for example. But if you already have one why not go and find some exciting action so as to test the camera's fastest speed? Photography is most enjoyable when you have equipment that extends slightly beyond your current capabilities or needs. As your skill grows, you will value the greater versatility your camera provides.

Good technique is here symbolized by a graphic image that suggests the photographer's sure-handed mastery of the camera's controls in framing and sharply focusing his subject.

Light, lens and film

The word photography means "drawing with light," a phrase that conveys both the creative and the chemical nature of the photographic process. A camera is simply a device for bringing together in a sharp image the light reflected from a scene and allowing it briefly to touch a film material so sensitive that the light leaves a trace, which can be developed into a finished picture.

To form an image, light has only to pass through a pinhole into a dark area and fall on a screen. The modern camera uses a lens and variable-size opening, or aperture, instead of a simple hole, and has a shutter that allows light in for fractions of time, which the photographer can control.

The advantage of a lens is that it can gather and focus light into a sharp, bright image. After collecting the light rays scattering out from every point on the subject, the lens bends them through precisely determined angles to meet again as points. These countless points, varying in color and brightness, form an image that is an exact copy of the subject's pattern of light. As shown in the diagram, the rays of light travel through the lens in such a way that this image arrives upside down and reversed, with light from the top of the subject brought to focus at the bottom of the image.

The film lies behind the lens on the plane where the light rays form a sharp image when the lens is focused for distant subjects. As a subject gets closer to the camera, its sharp image falls farther and farther behind the lens; hence, the lens must be moved forward in order to keep the image in focus on the film.

When the photographer opens the shutter, light from the subject begins to act on an emulsion coating on the film that contains crystals of silver halides. These salts of silver are extremely light-sensitive. They darken when exposed to light, much as skin tans in sunlight – but infinitely quicker. The light triggers a chemical change in the salts so that they start to form microscopic grains of black silver. Where more light strikes the film, more crystals are triggered. This process, however, is not visible to the naked eye, and the film requires chemical development before an image of the black silver pattern appears. The lightest areas of the subject – such as the sky – look black because they caused most silver to form, while shadow areas that sent no light to the film appear blank. The result is a *negative* image, which can be reversed in printing to make a *positive* image – recreating the tones (and with color films, the colors) of the original scene.

Anatomy of a camera

The parts of a camera, reduced to a schematic form, show in essence what a simple apparatus it is – a box for gathering and forming an image of the subject. Cameras come in many different shapes and sizes, but they all operate on the basic principles shown below.

Lens   Aperture and iris diaphragm   Shutter   Film

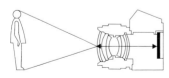

The lens brings the image into sharp focus on the film. Moving the lens forward or back changes the lens-to-film distance, focusing near or far subjects.

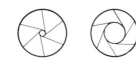

The aperture regulates the light entering the camera, usually by means of an iris diaphragm. This is a continuously variable ring of overlapping metal blades.

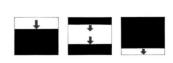

The shutter controls the length of time light falls onto the film. A common type exposes the film through an opening between two blinds that travel across the film.

The film, held flat at the focal plane, receives the image and records it. The film is wound on after each exposure, permitting a number of shots on each roll.

The camera you use

The variety of camera shapes and sizes may seem bewildering, but there is good reason for this diversity: cameras are designed for different tasks as well as different price brackets. Some are ideal for snapshots, and other, bigger cameras are more suited to applications that demand an image of exceptionally high quality.

Of all the different types, the 35mm camera is the most convenient compromise between image quality and ease of use. The term "35mm" refers to the width of the film, which comes in a long sprocketed strip loaded into a metal cassette. The actual size of a standard 35mm negative is $1 \times 1\frac{1}{2}$ inches – large enough to make quality prints as big as this page, but small enough for the camera that carries it to be reasonably compact.

The most versatile type of 35mm camera is the single lens reflex, or SLR for short. The term refers to the viewing system, which makes the camera extremely easy to use. A mirror reflects light from the single lens up to the viewfinder and shows exactly what is going to appear on film. Focusing and composing the picture is thus made simple. What makes the SLR so versatile is that its lens is removable and can be replaced by others that give different views or perform specialized tasks.

In addition to the SLR, there are other 35mm cameras. Single use cameras come ready loaded with film and can be used only once. Compact cameras have a fixed lens, and a direct viewfinder which gives *approximately* the same view as the camera lens. Most compacts are fully automated and are very easy to use. Hybrid cameras combine the fixed lens and point-and-shoot simplicity of a compact with the through-the-lens (TTL) viewing of an SLR camera.

Medium and large format cameras use film formats larger than 35mm. These cameras produce top quality images and are favoured by professional photographers.

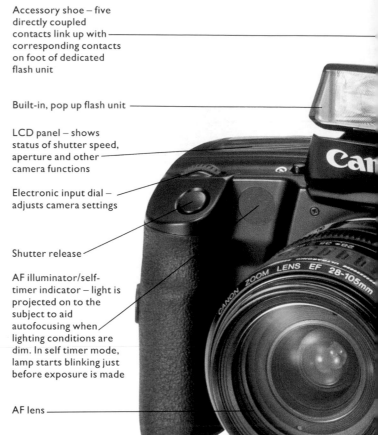

Accessory shoe – five directly coupled contacts link up with corresponding contacts on foot of dedicated flash unit

Built-in, pop up flash unit

LCD panel – shows status of shutter speed, aperture and other camera functions

Electronic input dial – adjusts camera settings

Shutter release

AF illuminator/self-timer indicator – light is projected on to the subject to aid autofocusing when lighting conditions are dim. In self timer mode, lamp starts blinking just before exposure is made

AF lens

35mm SLR

The distinctive body shape of the 35mm SLR is due to its viewing system. The camera is instantly recognizable by the central hump, housing the viewing prism and eyepiece. Modern SLRs are made from lightweight metal and plastic materials, but they still incorporate a reflex mirror behind the lens, so they are generally bigger and heavier than direct vision cameras such as compacts. SLRs range from basic, manually operated types to highly sophisticated electronically controlled models like the one shown here. Modern versions provide advanced features such as accurate autofocus systems and built-in motordrives. Even the simplest, however, incorporates a light-measuring system to advise on exposure.

SLR viewing system

The mirror and pentaprism in an SLR camera (left) let you see the image formed by the lens exactly as it will fall on the film. Light passing through the lens is reflected by the mirror onto a focusing screen, positioned at the same distance from the lens as is the film. This image is then converted by a five-sided prism (the pentaprism) so it can be viewed right way up and right way round. The mirror flips up out of the way when the shutter is released, thus allowing the light to reach the film.

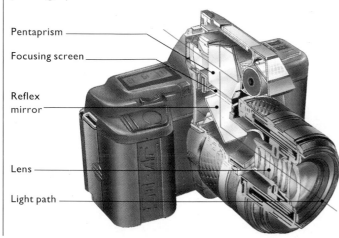

Pentaprism

Focusing screen

Reflex mirror

Lens

Light path

Function buttons and second electronic input dial on back of camera

Shooting mode selector – sets exposure mode

Lens release button

Manual focusing ring

Built-in, pop-up flash

Zoom control – used to alter focal length of zoom lens

Fixed zoom lens

Contoured handgrip

Hybrid 35mm camera

These cameras bridge the gap between the versatility offered by 35mm SLRs and the point-and-shoot simplicity of compact cameras – hence, they are commonly referred to as 'bridge cameras'. They are built around a fixed AF zoom lens, with an extensive focal length range, and are characterized by their space age styling. The self-contained design of hybrid cameras incorporates a built-in flash unit and motordrive and an array of advanced exposure modes and metering patterns.

Single use 35mm camera

These inexpensive cameras comprise a 35mm film housed in a small box, which is fitted with a basic film advance control and a fixed aperture, plastic lens on the front. When the film is finished, you send the camera to the lab. You get a set of prints back but not the camera. Exposure is fixed and exposure errors are corrected at the printing stage where possible.

Compact camera

Lightweight and fully automated, compacts are perfect for snapshots. Some models have a single focal length lens – usually a moderately wide angle, which gives an extensive field of view and great depth of field. Others have dual lenses, giving you a choice between a wide angle and a short telephoto. However, the most versatile compacts, like the one shown above, sport fixed zoom lenses. You can set any focal length within a limited range, and the size of the image in the viewfinder changes accordingly. Some models let you shoot long thin pictures, by selecting a panoramic mode.

63

What to do first

Nothing is more disappointing than taking a whole series of pictures and then discovering that the film did not wind through the camera because of incorrect loading in the first place. Happily, the automatic loading mechanisms of most modern cameras make this a rare occurrence, but it can still happen if you don't take sufficient care.

With an unfamiliar camera, always read the instructions to acquaint yourself with the layout and operation of the controls. This is especially important with older cameras like the one in the diagram at the bottom of the page. Loading newer cameras is usually simple, but you should always do it in the shade. Cassettes of 35mm film are not entirely light-proof and direct sun can spoil the first few pictures.

Once you have dropped the cassette into the film compartment you need only draw out the film leader across the camera until it reaches an index mark close to the take-up spool. Closing the camera back advances the film to the first frame, and you are ready to take pictures. Before you do so, though, you should check that the film is loaded correctly, and that there is sufficient battery power. Most cameras have indicators to verify that there are no problems, as shown on the right, and on many the shutter will not fire if the film is loaded incorrectly. However, if your camera is an older model that lacks a film advance symbol, take a look at the rewind knob each time the film advances. If your film is loaded correctly, the rewind knob will turn after each picture.

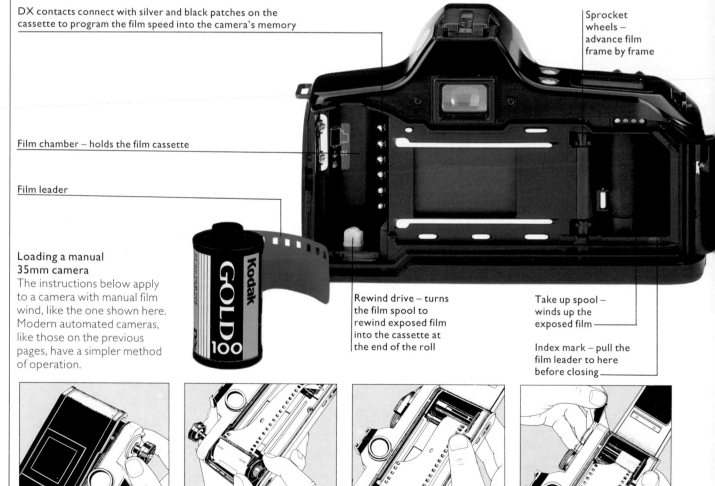

DX contacts connect with silver and black patches on the cassette to program the film speed into the camera's memory

Sprocket wheels – advance film frame by frame

Film chamber – holds the film cassette

Film leader

Loading a manual 35mm camera
The instructions below apply to a camera with manual film wind, like the one shown here. Modern automated cameras, like those on the previous pages, have a simpler method of operation.

Rewind drive – turns the film spool to rewind exposed film into the cassette at the end of the roll

Take up spool – winds up the exposed film

Index mark – pull the film leader to here before closing

1–In the shade, hold the camera firmly by the lens and pull up the rewind knob to open the camera back. Keep the knob raised.

2–Place the film in the left-hand chamber, then push in the rewind knob, turning it until it clicks firmly down into place.

3–Turn the film lip forward and insert the tongue into one of the slits in the take-up spool. Fit the bottom row of holes over the sprockets.

4–Next, click the shutter and wind on to ensure that the sprockets begin to engage both top and bottom rows of perforations.

Viewfinder displays

A few cameras provide the photographer with no viewfinder information at all, but most have at least an under/overexposure warning and show the shutter speed. This diagram shows a typical viewfinder display on an autofocus SLR.

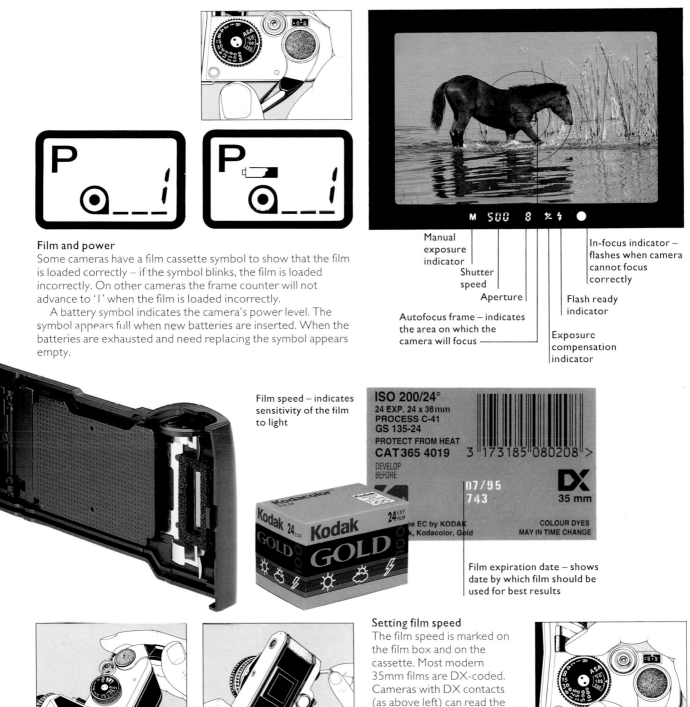

Manual exposure indicator

Shutter speed

Aperture

Autofocus frame – indicates the area on which the camera will focus

In-focus indicator – flashes when camera cannot focus correctly

Flash ready indicator

Exposure compensation indicator

Film and power

Some cameras have a film cassette symbol to show that the film is loaded correctly – if the symbol blinks, the film is loaded incorrectly. On other cameras the frame counter will not advance to 'I' when the film is loaded incorrectly.

A battery symbol indicates the camera's power level. The symbol appears full when new batteries are inserted. When the batteries are exhausted and need replacing the symbol appears empty.

Film speed – indicates sensitivity of the film to light

ISO 200/24°
24 EXP. 24 x 36mm
PROCESS C-41
GS 135-24
PROTECT FROM HEAT
CAT 365 4019
DEVELOP BEFORE

07/95
743

3 173185 080208

DX
35 mm

COLOUR DYES
MAY IN TIME CHANGE

Film expiration date – shows date by which film should be used for best results

Kodacolor GOLD Kodak 24 EXP. GOLD

Setting film speed

The film speed is marked on the film box and on the cassette. Most modern 35mm films are DX-coded. Cameras with DX contacts (as above left) can read the DX code and set the film speed automatically. But older 35mm cameras have a film speed dial (as shown on the right) that must be set manually to match the speed of the film loaded.

5–Close the camera back and continue advancing the film until the number for the first exposure appears in the exposure counter window.

6–To unload, release the rewind catch or button, lift the rewind crank, and turn it clockwise until it suddenly turns more easily.

Focusing the image

To achieve sharp images you need to focus the image on the film. To do this you move the lens forwards and backwards to change its distance from the film. Moving the lens farther away from the film brings into focus objects that are closer to the camera.

Except for some of the most basic compacts, all cameras offer some means of controlling the movement of the lens. Manual focus SLRs have a focusing control ring around the barrel of the lens. Turning this ring moves the lens backwards and forwards. Focusing aids at the center of the focusing screen help you judge when the image is in sharp focus. These are often a pair of semicircular prisms – which are together called a split image rangefinder – that split an unsharp image across the middle. When you turn the lens and bring the image into sharp focus, the prisms move together to form a perfectly aligned picture in the camera's viewfinder.

Around the split image rangefinder – or sometimes instead of it – is a ring of tiny prisms of a similar shape. These microprisms break up an unsharp image so that it appears shattered into countless fragments.

Autofocus cameras, as their name suggests, bring a subject to sharp focus automatically, though autofocus lenses for SLRs usually have a manual focusing control ring as well. In most compact cameras, autofocus relies on an infrared beam (or beams) emitted when you press the shutter release. This scans across the subject at the same time as the lens retracts – focusing from near to far. A sensor detects when the beam hits the subject and at the same moment the movement of the lens is stopped. This system, known as an "active" focusing system, works as well in darkness as in daylight.

The system used in most autofocus SLRs is "passive": it depends on sensors behind the lens which detect the sharpness of the image by measuring contrast. This system is very accurate, though it may struggle in poor light or with low contrast subjects – such as a clear sky or a flat wall in shade.

The advantage of the SLR system is that it can focus the lens at any distance. The "active" system is less accurate as it focuses the lens at a series of discrete distances or "steps" – as little as two or as many as 2,000. The more "steps" there are, the more accurately the lens is focused and the sharper the pictures are.

Whatever type of camera you use, in most pictures, a zone that looks acceptably sharp extends behind and in front of the plane you have focused on. The depth of this zone depends on several factors, including the size of the lens aperture, as pages 70-71 explain. But the diagram on the right, here, shows that an important factor is the distance of the subject from the lens. The closer you are to your subject, the more accurately you must focus the image.

The focusing control ring
Turning the wide, knurled ring focuses subjects at varying distances (indicated in feet and meters just under the ring). The ring moves the lens farther from the film for a subject only 3 ft away (left) than for far subjects (right), which are indicated by a symbol representing infinity (∞).

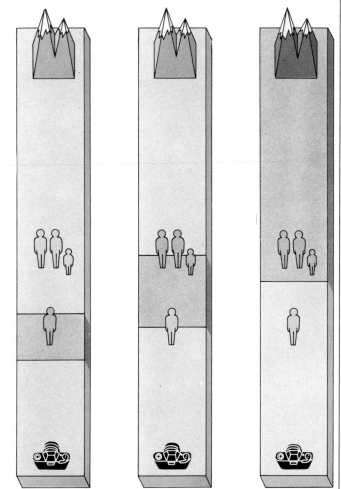

How much is in focus?
At close distances, only a very shallow part of a scene appears sharp (red zone above left). If you are taking a head-and-shoulders portrait, for example, at a range of a few feet, the background will blur (ocher area). The zone of sharp focus becomes progressively wider as you focus on more distant subjects (central group) until eventually the lens brings into focus objects in a zone stretching far back from the middle distance.

SLR manual focusing

The viewfinder contains a split circle in the center. When the subject is out of focus a straight line passing through this circle will be dislocated (right). In focus, the two split halves coincide (below).

Advanced autofocus modes

Most modern cameras, both 35mm SLR and compact, now have autofocus mechanisms that focus the lens for you. There are, however, many different types of autofocus mode, each designed for a different task.

In "one shot" autofocus mode, half pressing the shutter release activates the autofocus mechanism. The camera then focuses on the part of the image covered by the autofocus frame and locks the lens at this setting – provided the shutter release is kept half pressed. A viewfinder symbol indicates that the lens is correctly focused, and the shutter will not fire until the symbol appears.

In "continuous" mode, as long as the shutter release is kept half pressed, the camera constantly adjusts the lens to compensate for a subject's movements – up to the moment the shutter is released. The shutter can be released at any time.

"Predictive" autofocus is a more advanced version of continuous autofocus. The camera calculates the speed and direction in which the subject is travelling. It then predicts where the subject will be at the precise moment the shutter opens, and adjusts focus accordingly.

"Multizone" autofocus uses several focus frames – usually three or five, spread across the viewfinder – enabling you to focus on off-center subjects without moving the camera. The most sophisticated system, known as "eye controlled" autofocus, allows you to select focus frames simply by *looking* at them. A frame lights up when it is selected.

Moving subjects

Modern cameras with "predictive" autofocus mode can focus accurately on fast moving subjects like this skier (left). But for other autofocus cameras a rapid subject can be a problem. The solution may be to pre-focus on a spot in front of the subject and release the shutter just before the subject reaches this point.

Off-center subjects

Cameras with "multizone" autofocus cope well with off-center subjects. But cameras with a central focus frame only (as above) are easily fooled into focusing on the background rather than on the subject. The solution is to put the autofocus frame over the subject, lock the autofocus, then reframe the picture before finally taking the shot.

The shutter

The shutter is the basic picture-taking control on a camera. Releasing it smoothly, at just the right moment, makes all the difference to a shot. Never hurry – the secret of sharp, well-timed pictures is to be ready, and anticipate the moment, squeezing the release gently when you feel everything in the viewfinder is perfect.

Choosing the right shutter speed is just as important. It affects both sharpness and exposure. The numbers on the shutter speed dial or LCD panel are called speeds, but they are actually exposure times – seconds and fractions of a second for which the shutter stays open, exposing the film to the image-forming light projected by the lens. For simplicity, 30 is used to mean 1/30 second, and 60 to mean 1/60 second. The higher the number, the faster the speed and the briefer the exposure. Doubling a shutter number – for example, from 30 to 60 – halves the exposure time. Most SLR cameras have a fastest shutter speed of 1/1000, 1/2000, 1/4000 or 1/8000, but SLRs with a top speed of 1/12,000 are available.

For a sharp picture, the fastest practical shutter speed is the safest to use, because the less time during which light from an image falls onto the film, the less time there is for any subject movement or camera shake to blur the photograph. Camera shake while the shutter is open is probably the commonest cause of disappointing pictures.

A safe working speed for handheld shots with a normal lens is 1/125 second – fast enough to stop camera shake and freeze all except rapid motion. Close-ups and shots with telephoto lenses need faster speeds – 1/250 or 1/500 second – and so do active scenes such as children playing.

In practice, the choice is often limited by the lighting – in dimmer light longer exposures are needed, and this makes it difficult to freeze movement. On dull days or indoors, speeds below 1/60 second may be required for an adequate picture, and then it is necessary to provide the camera with a support – if possible, use a tripod and a cable release.

At slow shutter speeds, any movement blurs the image. *In the picture below of a girl roller skating in a park, a speed of 1/30 dissolves her whole body into streaks of color.*

Setting shutter speed
Shutter speed is set using a variety of controls, depending on the camera make. Generally, an LCD panel shows the shutter speed chosen (1/4000 in this example). Older cameras have a dial to set the speed. Most of the more advanced cameras offer a choice of shutter speeds in the range 30 seconds to 1/8000, though a few models offer faster and slower speeds.

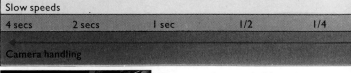

Slow speeds

4 secs	2 secs	1 sec	1/2	1/4

Camera handling

Slow speeds are suitable not only for static subjects but also when you want to suggest movement impressionistically. The lights of city traffic at night (left) have been blurred into vivid, rushing streaks by using a shutter speed of 1/4.

At medium speeds (here 1/125), there is still some blur, but it shows mainly in the hands and feet – the parts of the body that are moving at greatest speed.

Fast shutter speeds will freeze all movement. At 1/500, the girl's body, hands and feet are sharp, even though she is racing toward the camera at full tilt.

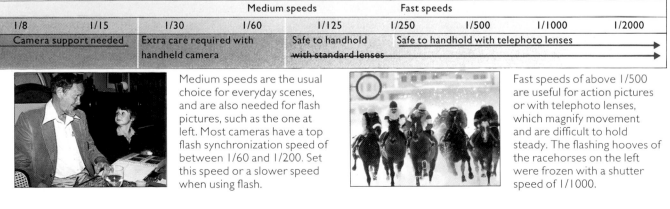

		Medium speeds		Fast speeds				
1/8	1/15	1/30	1/60	1/125	1/250	1/500	1/1000	1/2000
Camera support needed		Extra care required with handheld camera		Safe to handhold with standard lenses	Safe to handhold with telephoto lenses			

Medium speeds are the usual choice for everyday scenes, and are also needed for flash pictures, such as the one at left. Most cameras have a top flash synchronization speed of between 1/60 and 1/200. Set this speed or a slower speed when using flash.

Fast speeds of above 1/500 are useful for action pictures or with telephoto lenses, which magnify movement and are difficult to hold steady. The flashing hooves of the racehorses on the left were frozen with a shutter speed of 1/1000.

The aperture

The aperture is the opening of the lens through which light enters the camera. On all but the simplest cameras, you can increase or decrease the opening, usually by means of an iris diaphragm, and this is one of the principal ways of controlling how the picture will look. Widening the aperture allows more light to reach the film. Together with shutter speed (which controls the amount of time during which light can affect the film), this determines the exposure – the total amount of light that reaches the film. The other important function of the aperture is that it affects depth of field – the zone of sharp focus in a scene, extending from the nearest element that is sharp to the farthest. Because wrong focus is less noticeable if the effective lens area is reduced, depth of field increases as aperture size decreases.

Aperture is adjusted in a series of stops, each full stop doubling or halving the amount of light let in. These stops are arranged in a coded numerical series called f-numbers, running in a standard sequence f/1, f/1.4, f/2, f/2.8, f/4, f/5.6, f/8, f/11, f/16, f/22. Some cameras let you set the aperture in third stops or half stops – such as f/13, which indicates an aperture setting halfway between f/11 and f/16. The numbers get bigger as the aperture opening gets smaller. Thus, f/16 is a small aperture and lets in less light than f/2. The system ensures that the same f-number lets the same amount of light reach the film, irrespective of the size and type of lens you use.

A lens's lowest f-number indicates the largest aperture the lens can provide, often between f/1.4 and f/4. To let you view the subject clearly, modern lenses usually stay open at this maximum aperture until you press the shutter release, then the aperture "stops down" to the selected f-number. This means that while you view and focus on the subject, near and far objects may look fuzzy because the aperture has not yet stopped down and improved the depth of field. Many cameras have a depth of field preview button (below). When pressed, it alters the image in the viewfinder to show the actual extent of sharpness.

At maximum aperture, used for the picture below, *depth of field is very shallow. Only the main focused subject is sharp. Foreground and background are blurred.*

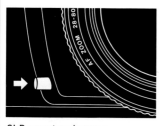

SLR preview button
This is often on, or by, the lens. You simply press it to preview the true depth of field of the aperture.

Aperture scale
The sequence of f-stops is shown at right, light being halved at each setting. The pictures below the scale show the effect on exposure if the aperture is reduced without slowing the shutter speed. By using a preview button, you can see the image darkening at each stop as the aperture steadily cuts the light admitted.

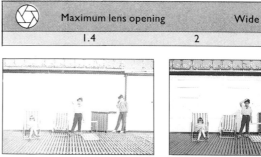

Maximum lens opening		Wide
1.4	2	2.8

f/2 Bright image,
shallow depth of field

f/2.8 One stop down

At a medium aperture, depth of field is greater. The farthest child and most of the background are sharp. But the boy in the foreground is still out of focus.

At minimum aperture, depth of field is so great that even the foreground boy is sharp. The shot needed a slow shutter speed at this aperture, so any movement would have blurred.

	Medium			Small		Minimum lens opening
4	5.6	8	11	16	22	

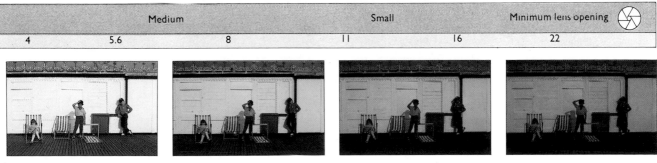

f/4 Two stops down

f/5.6 Three stops down

f/8 Four stops down

f/11 Five stops down, good depth of field

How lenses control the image

In its ability to capture and focus the image of a subject on film, the lens is the most important part of the camera. The size and appearance of the image can vary greatly according to the type of lens you are using. And as all 35mm SLRs can be fitted with interchangeable lenses, photographers need to understand some basic lens characteristic.

How much of the scene a lens can capture depends on its angle of view – the way it sees the subject in front of the camera. This is determined by the focal length of the lens – in simple terms the distance from the optical center of the lens to the film plane when focus is set to infinity. Focal length is marked on the front of the lens in millimeters, and this is how lenses are normally described – as 28mm, 50mm or 135mm lenses, for example. Most lenses are within a range from 18mm to about 600mm, although shorter and longer focal lengths can be obtained for more specialized purposes.

Lenses with short focal lengths can convey to the film more of a scene than the eye itself can see when looking through a frame the same size as the viewfinder. They do this by sharply bending the light passing through them, making each object in the scene appear smaller than the eye would see it and, by means of this optical shrinkage, fitting more objects into the frame. For this reason, lenses of short focal length are called wide-angle lenses. The most extreme of them is the so-called fisheye lens, which produces bizarre distortions by compressing an exceptionally wide view onto the relatively small format of the film. At the other end of the scale, telephoto lenses – with long focal lengths – bend the light from the subject relatively little, and produce an enlarged image of a small part of the view, as does a telescope.

From a single camera position, you can thus produce completely different views of the subject by

1 – A 28mm wide-angle lens takes in a broad view of the subject, but makes the distant buildings appear smaller than they would to the eye. This view of the Manhattan skyline from Liberty Island includes a large expanse of the stormy sky that loomed over the city when the shot was taken – and links near and far elements of the scene. But New York's famous skyline looks relatively insignificant.

2 – A 50mm standard lens renders the scene more as the eye would see it. The photographer aimed higher to keep in much of the sky but exclude the foreground. The lens helps to emphasize the city skyline, and the view is relatively wide.

using different lenses. With a wide-angle lens, a human figure can be shown as part of an extensive landscape, or you can close in on the face alone with a telephoto lens. The enormous flexibility gained by having interchangeable lenses is one of the great advantages of the 35mm SLR camera. On the other hand, individual lenses are expensive and also heavy to carry around. One solution is the zoom lens, which has an infinitely variable focal length within a set range, allowing you to achieve a variety of framings and subject enlargements with a single lens. But be careful; top quality zooms are very expensive and they usually have smaller maximum apertures than do equivalent lenses of fixed focal length. Zoom lenses are also heavier than similar lenses of fixed focal length because of their complex construction, and so may be more difficult to handle. The six pages that follow introduce the major types of lenses and the creative uses to which they can be put.

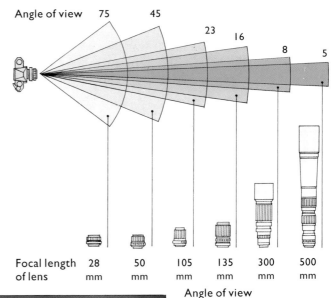

| Angle of view | 75 | 45 | 23 | 16 | 8 | 5 |
| Focal length of lens | 28 mm | 50 mm | 105 mm | 135 mm | 300 mm | 500 mm |

Angle of view

The lenses shown above with their angles of view are those most commonly used with 35mm SLRs. Note that the lens with the widest angle of view requires only a short body. Longer lenses can reach out farther to close in on (and enlarge) distant details. But as the focal length increases, the extent of the view decreases, both in width and in height. Cameras with film formats larger than 35mm require lenses of longer focal length to achieve the same results, because more enlargement is needed to cover the larger area of the film itself.

3 – A 135mm telephoto lens brings forward the buildings in the same scene, making the twin towers of the World Trade Center the dominant subject. The sky now takes up a much smaller part of the frame, and the skyline is reduced in width.

The size we see

The 35mm SLR camera comes fitted with a 50mm lens (or sometimes 55mm) – the so-called standard lens. Many photographers never use any other lens, and still take perfectly good pictures.

The most striking feature of the image produced by a standard lens is the naturalness of its perspective. Because wide-angle lenses take in a broad view of the subject, they actually appear to reduce the scale of distant objects in relation to those in the foreground, thus exaggerating the perspective effect by which objects appear smaller the farther away they are. Telephoto lenses have the reverse effect, appearing to compress objects together despite the distance between them. The standard lens, on the other hand, reproduces the scene with its perspective much as the eye sees it. In a sense, photography is most objective with a standard lens – the camera shows the world essentially as we see it.

Because standard lenses are produced in large quantities, they are relatively cheap. They are also extremely versatile. They are suitable for near and distant subjects, accurately focusing subjects at a considerable distance and within two feet of the lens. And they can be used in low light – or with fast shutter speeds in action shots – because they have wide maximum apertures: f/1.8 is common and f/1.4 is not unusual. Taking good pictures with standard lenses needs skill, however. As there is no strong special photographic feature such as dramatic magnification to compensate for poor composition, the image can easily appear bland. More than with any other lens, you must frame the picture accurately and compose it carefully.

Street portraits look more natural when taken with a standard lens – the distortion-free images it forms closely resemble the world as seen with our eyes.

The standard lens
The photographer's work-horse, the 50mm or 55mm lens can give good definition, even in failing light.

A red bicycle, the same shade as the nearby door, establishes a simple but vibrant pattern of line and color. For uncomplicated compositions such as this, the standard lens is ideal.

A tanned back says "summer sun" more eloquently than might a traditional beach scene. The close-focusing capability of the standard lens allowed the photographer to frame the image tightly and eliminate surrounding clutter.

Widening the view

Although a standard lens shows natural perspective, you need a lens of much shorter focal length to get breadth of view. The view of a standard lens is restricted to a viewing angle of about 45°, and to overcome this restriction, you need a lens that can fit more into the same frame – a wide-angle lens. With a 35mm SLR camera, any focal length shorter than about 35mm gives a wide-angle view, although the effects become really noticeable only at 28mm or shorter: many photographers use 35mm lenses in place of a standard lens. Focal lengths shorter than 24mm are available. But while compressing such a broad field of view onto the film format, very wide-angle lenses create distortion, and the more extreme of them are best considered as interesting special-effects devices.

Distortion will be most obvious with scenes involving straight lines, as in architectural photographs.

The most obvious practical use of a wide-angle lens is for pictures in which interesting details cover a wide angle in relation to where you are standing. If you want to show most of your living room in one photograph, for example, your eyes, with an angle of view approaching 160° from left to right, may see the whole room. But it may be impossible to move back far enough to fit everything into the viewfinder frame. A wide-angle lens will help by reducing the image of the objects in the room and squeezing more of them onto the film. In the same way, a wide-angle lens allows you to frame an exterior scene effectively with foreground objects near the frame

Sweeping perspectives and an impressive sense of space give a dramatic look to landscapes shot with a wide-angle lens. Taking advantage of the distortion inherent in a 20mm lens, the photographer of the desert road on the left has turned his picture into a striking landscape, with the road itself forming a shape of startling impact.

Cramped space makes it impossible to move back far enough to show a subject like this adequately without a wide-angle lens. The 35mm lens used here was wide enough to allow the photographer to close in on a furniture restorer and the instrument he is polishing, yet still show his surroundings.

Framed by an arch, and shaded by citrus trees, these Portuguese women make a fascinating folk tableau for the camera. By composing the picture in order to exploit the wide angle of view and great depth of field of the 28mm lens he was using, the photographer was able to include much of the surroundings, and to identify the location as a quiet courtyard. A standard lens would have shown only the group, losing much of the intimacy of this image.

edges, as in the shot here taken through an archway. The result is often to draw the viewer into the picture, creating a feeling of involvement that can give photographs taken with a wide-angle lens a strong sense of immediacy.

As a most useful side-effect, lenses of short focal length produce greater depth of field than do standard lenses at the same aperture. This makes them very useful in poor light and in situations where there is little time to make fine adjustments to the focus. When you are photographing general street scenes with a manual focus camera, for example, a wide-angle lens will let you point the camera and shoot without delaying the moment to adjust the focusing ring.

24mm

28mm

35mm

Wide-angle lenses
These three lenses, which have focal lengths of 24mm, 28mm and 35mm, outwardly resemble standard lenses. But the likeness ends as soon as you fit one to your camera and look through the viewfinder. Cramped views expand, and at small apertures the depth of field makes focusing less critical.

Concentrating the view

Distant subjects that look good in the viewfinder often seem disappointing in the final print, because the attractive details that initially caught the eye occupy only a small area in the middle of the frame. Moving closer is sometimes the answer, but if you are photographing a football game, for example, you cannot intrude on to the playing area. The solution is to use a telephoto lens. This has an effect opposite to that of a wide-angle lens – instead of taking in a wider field of view than a standard lens, it records a much smaller area, and magnifies the subject.

The degree of magnification depends on the focal length of the lens. A 100mm telephoto has a focal length double that of a standard lens, so it doubles the scale at which the eye would perceive a subject. At the same time, the lens's horizontal field of view is half as wide as that of a standard lens.

The most popular telephotos have focal lengths of between 85 and 250mm. The longer focal lengths, although powerful, are much more difficult to handle and to focus. Those of 400mm and longer can pick out subject details missed by the naked eye but require tripod support.

Aside from their magnifying effect, all telephoto lenses have several other common characteristics. The most dramatic of these is the compression of distance that they appear to cause. If you look at a row of objects of equal height and equally spaced – such as telegraph poles – receding into the distance, you will notice that the distant ones seem more tightly packed. When you photograph this scene with a telephoto lens, only the distant poles are included in the frame, and so the picture appears flattened out with its different planes packed together. For example, in the shot of the Grand Canyon on the opposite page, a scene that stretches away from the camera for several miles has been foreshortened startlingly, because a long lens has eliminated the foreground.

Another important characteristic of a telephoto lens is that it gives less depth of field than does a standard lens. As a result, when the lens is focused on a nearby object, the background is unsharp – a useful way of concentrating attention on the principal area of interest. Portraiture with telephoto lenses is often effective for this reason – and also because you do not need to crowd your subject to get a detailed head-and-shoulders shot.

Telephoto lenses

Telephoto lenses magnify the image, filling the frame with a subject that may look like an insignificant detail when seen through a standard lens. These three lenses have focal lengths of 135mm, 200mm and 400mm, magnifying the image 2.7, 4 and 8 times respectively.

400mm

200mm

135mm

Pleasing portraits are easier with a telephoto – its shallow depth of field puts background distractions out of focus. At the same time, magnification of the image allows you to move back to a more comfortable working distance, thus eliminating perspective distortions.

The majesty of landscape is often missing from pictures taken with a standard lens. A telephoto can restore the sense of scale and drama – as in the picture here of the Grand Canyon, taken with a 200mm lens.

The thick of the action at a sports event usually can be captured effectively only with a telephoto lens. The photographer of the football game opposite used a 400mm lens to get close to a player weaving through tacklers on the far side of the field.

Recording everything sharply

More often than not you will want your entire image to be sharp from foreground to background – to give a figure a sense of location, for example, to link foreground and background elements, or merely to record the whole of a view. The simplest way to maximize depth of field is to stop down the lens. Stopping down means reducing the aperture of the lens, and the smaller the aperture you use, the greater the depth of field in your photograph. Stopped down to f/16, for example, a standard lens focused on a subject 15 feet away will record sharply everything beyond about eight feet, whereas with the aperture widened to f/2, only the subject itself will be sharply focused, the background and foreground appearing blurred.

Stopping down the lens requires that you also slow the shutter speed to give sufficient exposure. Unless the light is bright, this may limit your freedom to choose an aperture small enough to gain the depth of field you want. Fast film can help or, if the subject is static, you may be able to shoot at a slow shutter speed with the camera steadied – preferably on a tripod. To check how much of your picture will be sharp at a given aperture, you can either refer to the depth of field scale on the lens (see below left) or use the preview button. This closes the lens down to the f-stop you have chosen, allowing you to see through the viewfinder the zone of sharp focus in your image.

Two other factors control the extent to which you can record the whole picture sharply – the lens you use and the camera-to-subject distance. The shorter the focal length of your lens the greater the depth of field. Thus a wide-angle lens has advantages if you want the greatest near-to-far sharpness. Finally, you can extend sharpness by moving back from your subject, since depth of field increases with the distance between the camera and the subject.

Using the depth of field scale

A typical autofocus lens (below) has a focusing distance scale linked by engraved lines to pairs of f-numbers on a depth of field scale. From a chosen f-number, the left-hand line indicates the distance to the nearest point in sharp focus and the right-hand line indicates the farthest point.

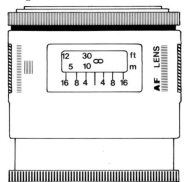

Above, the lens is focused on infinity (marked with a ∞ symbol on the distance scale) and the aperture set at f/8. The line from the "8" on the left points to 16 feet, showing that focus is sharp only beyond this distance. The "8" line on the right, which is well beyond the infinity symbol, indicates that there is depth of field to spare.

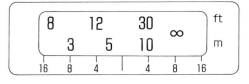

By turning the manual focusing ring to the right so that the ∞ symbol aligns with the "8" line on the right, infinity is still in focus. But depth of field now extends down to 10 feet, so more of the foreground is in focus.

The maternal bond between an ostrich and her eggs makes a striking composition. Focusing on the midground ensured that both were sharp despite the distance dividing them.

Isolating what is important

In photography, you often need to take special measures to focus attention on one center of interest – usually because there are distracting elements in front of or behind your main subject, and you may not be able to get near enough to your subject to cut out the unwanted details. When you are taking a candid portrait, for example, bright colors or strong shapes in the background or foreground may compete for attention with your chosen subject. In such circumstances the best way to simplify the image is to put intrusive elements out of focus by deliberately creating a shallow depth of field. Colors are toned down and shapes reduced to an unobtrusive blur when they are out of focus.

There are three ways of minimizing depth of field: using a wide aperture, a telephoto lens, or a close viewpoint. Just as you can stop down the lens to achieve maximum depth of field (overleaf), so you can deliberately open up the lens and choose the widest aperture possible to take advantage of the restricted focus it offers. Of course, using a wide aperture makes it crucial that you focus accurately on the part of the scene you want to be sharp, as any slight error will be noticeable. Because telephoto lenses have more limited depth of field than standard lenses, they are well suited for selective focusing, especially when set at a wide aperture. Finally, if the light is too bright for a very wide aperture to be feasible, remember that you can also throw a background out of focus by moving in close to your subject – depth of field is shallower in close-ups than at average focusing distances.

A face in a crowd can be made to stand out. Here, the photographer focused carefully on the girl, then opened up the lens to blur the foreground leaves and soften the background. The blurred elements serve both to emphasize the sharply focused face and to frame it.

Zoo portraits are often spoiled by cage bars and wire netting. Here, however, the photographer concentrated attention on the main subject by holding the camera close to the cage and using a wide aperture to cut depth of field. This throws the bars and netting out of focus, making them less noticeable.

A girl balancing on the bar of her sports bicycle totally dominates the picture here, because a telephoto lens set at a wide aperture has been used in order to soften the intrusive colors and shapes in the busy street behind her. Shooting with a telephoto lens is also a simple way of filling the frame with your main subject without having to get too close.

The right film

In selecting what kind of film to put in the camera, the broad choice lies between film for color prints, for color slides or for pictures in black-and-white (overleaf). Within these categories are many different types of film – it is easier to take successful shots if the film chosen matches the subject and lighting conditions as precisely as possible.

The most important property of a film is its sensitivity to light – the film speed. Slow films need much more light to form a usable image than do fast films, which are highly sensitive. This means that you can more easily take pictures in dim light with fast film. In brighter light, fast film allows you to select a fast shutter speed or a small aperture if needed. However, fast films have one drawback: the grains that make up the image have to be large so that they react quickly to a limited amount of light, and when the picture is blown up they show as gritty texture. Slow films have smaller grains and can record finer detail, but unless the light is bright, they may force the photographer to use an unsuitably slow shutter speed or too wide an aperture. In average daylight, films of medium or medium-fast speed offer a good compromise. Fast films are an advantage in poor light or for action photographs requiring fast shutter speeds. Slow films are useful for static, detailed subjects, such as still-life or architecture.

Film speed used to be indicated by an ASA (American Standards Association) or DIN (Deutsche Industrie Norm) number, but nowadays it is designated by the ISO (International Standards Organization) system whereby the ASA number appears first, then the DIN number. Thus, ISO 100/21° (or simply ISO 100) indicates ASA 100 or 21°DIN – a medium speed. Each doubling or halving of the ISO number indicates a doubling or halving of speed, changing the exposure required by one full stop on either the aperture or shutter speed controls.

For fine detail, as in this shot of a tub of chilies in a market stall, slow film is best. The Kodachrome 25 film for slides used here has extremely fine grain (seen in the inset microscopic enlargement).

In average light, medium-speed film works well, needing not too wide an aperture and showing little grain (inset). This picture of the interior of a partly inflated hot-air balloon was shot on Ektachrome 64 film for slides.

Film speed
The film speed rating is clearly marked on the box, as at left. Kodak Ektar 100 film – a medium film for color prints – takes its name from the ISO speed rating, which is numerically the same as the old ASA rating. New cameras set the speed automatically when you load the film. On older cameras, you need to set a control to the correct ISO number (bottom left). The guide to film speeds (right) shows the range and differing sensitivities.

	ISO	Slow		Medium	
Color prints		25			100
Color slides		25	50	64	100
Black-and-white		25	50		100

Slow films (ISO 25-50) are the ideal choice whenever fine detail and saturated color is important, provided the light is bright or you can set a long exposure.

Medium speed films (ISO 64-200) are designed for everyday photography. They offer fine quality results, but can be used under overcast lighting conditions.

Dim light or fast action calls for fast film. There was just enough light on this building at dusk for a hand-held picture on Ektachrome 400 film. In big enlargements, however, grain is noticeable, as the inset shows.

			Fast					Ultra Fast		
(125)	160	200		400			1000	1600	(3200)
	160	200	320	400	(640)	800		1600	
125				400				1600	3200

Fast films (ISO 320-800) are useful in a wide range of situations, from poor light outdoors to artificial light indoors. Image quality is high with modern films.

Ultra fast films (ISO 1000-3200) tend to give grainy images, but are useful when light is very dim. With these films, you can take pictures by candlelight.

Note to table: brackets signify that films at this speed rating are available only from manufacturers other than Kodak.

Choosing black-and-white film

Why should anyone use black-and-white film? After all, it is now only slightly cheaper than color and the bright hues of nature seem a lot to sacrifice. But black-and-white clearly does have a great appeal, and is the chosen medium of many good photographers. What this film lacks in color, it gains in dramatic impact. Whereas the variety and vibrancy of color sometimes complicate the appearance of a scene, black-and-white has a graphic simplicity that is well shown in the picture on the opposite page – an ability to convey mood, form, and pattern solely in tones of light and dark. You can learn important lessons in photography by using this film, because it is one step farther removed from the real world. Without color you can more easily concentrate on composing with light, developing a new and valuable way of seeing the world around you.

Black-and-white film has other, more practical advantages. Processing is simple, allowing both development and printing to be carried out at home with relative ease. The equipment needed is neither expensive nor complicated. And home processing allows total control over the final image, including subtle adjustment to the quality of the print.

Black-and-white film is available in a wide range of speeds which adds to its versatility. Slow film (ISO 25) is useful for copying prints onto a new negative or for photography requiring fine detail. Using such film, big enlargements can be made without graininess appearing. At the other end of the scale, ultra-fast film of ISO 3200 will cope with very dim light or fast-moving subjects.

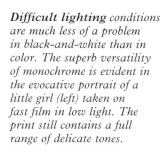

Manipulating prints from a black-and-white negative is relatively easy. Here, selective cropping and enlargement during printing have produced several quite different portraits of a boy from a single negative.

Difficult lighting conditions are much less of a problem in black-and-white than in color. The superb versatility of monochrome is evident in the evocative portrait of a little girl (left) taken on fast film in low light. The print still contains a full range of delicate tones.

Tone and texture create a powerful abstract image in this high-contrast picture of sand dunes (right). Black-and-white concentrates attention on such qualities.

Choosing color film

Most photographers simply want the film they use to record accurately the colors they see. Thus it may seem surprising that such a range of color film is available. For 35mm cameras, there are several dozen types of daylight and indoor films. The reason for this diversity is that each film has its own characteristics, and you may want to choose different films for different purposes.

The initial choice, of course, lies between films for slides (transparencies) or for negatives from which you can make prints. Beyond this, a film's sensitivity to light is the main consideration. Fast films are very sensitive, and give the photographer great versatility, but slower, less sensitive films have other advantages. For example, they provide a good range of tones between light and dark. And because they make use of finer grains of light-sensitive silver salts to form an image, they can look sharper and are less grainy in big enlargements than photographs taken on faster film.

Although grain size is a consideration when choosing color film, the film's color rendition is often more important. A photograph of the same scene taken on different types of film will vary slightly but distinctly in color, as the pictures below show. One film may record reds with special intensity. Another may distinguish more clearly colors that are closely similar. Yet another film may give the picture a warmer or cooler appearance overall – this is particularly noticeable in neutral color areas such as black, white and gray, and in skin tones. In photographs, it is often in the skin tones that we are most sensitive to variations in color values and most disturbed by unnaturalness.

Variations of color are usually quite subtle, and are most obvious when you make comparisons between slide films; the printing process tends to reduce the differences between negative films. In general, photographers form their own preferences for color film. The best way to make a choice is to try out a number of films, and decide which you like most. You may even want to use two different films, choosing for portraits a type that produces very natural skin tones, but preferring a different film for landscapes, where you may feel that the rendition of blues and greens is more important. The difference in the qualities of the blues is one of the features of the color films shown below.

The color characteristics of film
This garden still-life incorporates a wide range of colors. Shot on different types of slide film, the colors show slight but distinct differences – for example, in some the blue is stronger, in others the red. The green is particularly strong in the image second from right. However there is no "best", because color judgments are largely subjective.

Subtle colors and flowing movement emphasize the grace and beauty of dance. Here, the photographer chose fast film to cope with the dim light of the rehearsal room. This film has helped to soften the colors.

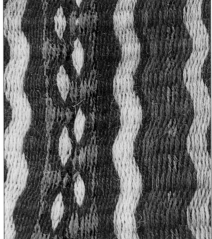

A vivid piece of woven fabric relies for its impact on the juxtaposition of primary colors. The photographer took the picture with slow transparency film, which has moderate contrast and good color fidelity, suited to the reproduction of vibrant hues.

How color film works

Color print film is like a layer cake (above) made of gelatin containing grains of silver salts. Each layer records a different part of the visible spectrum – red, green or blue light. Processing creates a silver image where light was absorbed in each layer. At the same time, a dye image appears in color exactly opposite to the color for which the layer is sensitized. For example, the blue-sensitive layer forms a yellow dye image. After bleach and fix have removed the silver image, the dye layers (visible in the magnified cross-section above) form the negative from which a positive print is made. Processing of color slides is more complex because the film must form a positive picture. During processing, a second development introduces transparent dyes that form the image, subtracting appropriate colors from the light that passes through the slide.

Slide film

To achieve precision and brilliance of color, many photographers prefer to use color slide film – often called transparency or color reversal film. Because this produces a positive film image directly, without an intermediate printing process, any adjustment the photographer makes to the camera's controls leads directly to a corresponding change in the appearance of the final picture.

Although color slides need projection or enlargement to be seen properly, they display great brilliance and color saturation. We see slides by transmitted, rather than reflected, light. Therefore, the range of brightness is higher – a slide usually has more snap than a print (see overleaf).

This impact derives partly from the higher contrast of slide films – they allow little latitude for over- or underexposure. On a dull day, or under flat lighting, this is an advantage, but on a bright sunny day, when the shadows are very dark, and the highlights bright, high contrast can prove a problem. At worst you can lose highlight and shadow detail altogether, depending on how you set the exposure.

As a general rule, blank highlights – for example pale, washed-out features in a portrait – are more likely to spoil a picture than are murky shadows. For this reason, if you are uncertain about the light, some underexposure of color slide film is better than overexposure.

Regular users of color transparency film often deliberately underexpose all their pictures to take account of this – usually by a third or half a stop. Even in low or flat lighting conditions, slight underexposure leads to richer, more saturated colors. You can also underexpose by setting your camera's film speed control to a slightly higher speed – say ISO 80 if you are using ISO 64 film.

When the contrast between highlights and shadows is very high – in strong sunlight or when shooting into the sun – bracketing exposures increases the chance of getting just the picture you want. For the sunset pictures shown below, the photographer used this simple technique, making exposures at intervals of one stop above and below the setting indicated by the camera's meter.

The sunset *looks different in this picture than in the three on the right, because the photographer varied or bracketed the exposure so that he could choose the best. The image above received two stops more exposure than the meter indicated. The result is pale but pleasing, with a satisfying balance of tones.*

One stop overexposure *gives the best balanced result. There is more detail in the sand spit and clouds compared with the pictures on the right.*

Underexposure of color slide film can add to color saturation and avoid the burned-out appearance of sunlit highlights. For the picture of a flower bed (right), the photographer deliberately set the camera to give half a stop less exposure than the meter indicated. The inset shows the "correct" exposure setting (above).

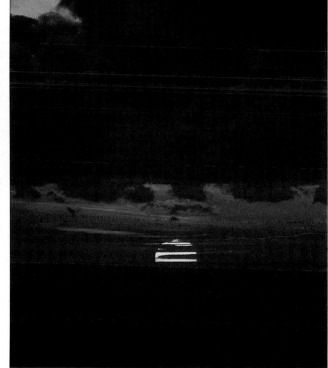

At the metered setting, most of the cloud and sea areas are left as broad masses, but in compensation the red sky is particularly rich.

One stop underexposure produces an image that loses almost all the detail, but is still acceptable because of its dramatic effect.

Print film

While slide films have the advantage of brilliance and color intensity, you need to project them onto a screen or use a small viewer to see them at their best. Many people prefer to see their pictures in the form of a print which they can hold in their hands. And because of the brilliance of the original, a paper print made from a transparency rarely seems as satisfactory. If your principal aim is prints, then color negative film may be your best choice.

Because a print is viewed in different conditions to a slide, its colors may appear more muted, and some photographers prefer to work with color negative film because they consider that the hues and tones of a print have more subtlety than those of a slide. Another significant difference is the low contrast of a negative compared with a slide. If you hold a negative up to the light it will look relatively dull. However, because the negative is only an intermediate step on the way to a print, low contrast is not the disadvantage it may seem. It means that negative film can be corrected for some over- or underexposure. As a result the film is ideal for

simple cameras that do not have sophisticated ways of avoiding exposure errors. Even when loaded into an SLR camera, negative film needs less care in assessing exposure than does slide film because to a certain extent exposure errors can be corrected during printing.

Printing a color negative can be much more than just the mechanical process of reversing colors to their normal hues. First, a color-correcting mask that gives the negative an orange tint has to be removed. Then, and more significantly, printing provides the opportunity to control selectively the overall or local color of the picture, and to correct for errors in color balance as well as exposure.

For the many photographers who print their own negatives in home darkrooms, the printing process can, in fact, be just as creative as actually taking photographs. Even if you do not have a home darkroom, you can exert some measure of control over the appearance of the final print by examining a contact sheet (see opposite) and giving appropriate directions to the color laboratory.

The unreal hues of a color negative (right) are little help in judging the final color of the print (above). Part of the problem is the orange dye mask that covers the whole of the negative. This helps to produce more accurate colors in the print, but makes interpretation of the reversed colors more difficult. The best general guide to how a negative will print is its density. A thin negative – one that is underexposed – has little visible detail and will produce a dark, muddy print. By comparison, a dense negative – one that is overexposed – creates fewer problems for the printer.

Purple in the negative will appear as yellow in the print – the orange mask has combined with blue (the complementary of yellow) to give the purple appearance.

Yellow in the negative also forms its complementary color – blue – on the print. The orange mask distorts yellow only slightly.

Green in the negative will print as red – the gloves in the girl's pocket.

A contact sheet, on which an entire roll of film has been printed, provides you with a convenient working guide to the appearance of all the pictures on the roll. Some laboratories can make a contact sheet, from which you can then choose which images to enlarge, say how they should be cropped to improve the composition, and decide if color correction is needed. From this roll, the photographer picked out the image of the boat, and asked the printer to bring out an overall warm color and crop the picture on the left-hand side. Both these changes would be simple to make in a home darkroom.

MAKE LIGHT
WORK FOR YOU

Modern cameras simplify exposure control. Their automatic systems of measuring and regulating the light that enters the camera do most of the work for you. But the camera will not always get it right, because no amount of technological wizardry or computerized circuitry can produce just the picture you want in every situation. Camera systems work to fixed rules, whereas exposing the film often involves a creative choice. In the final analysis, you must yourself decide how you would like the picture to look and, if necessary, overrule the automatic system.

A good camera metering system aims to provide an exposure that is technically correct – one that offers a compromise between the amount of light needed for dark and light areas of the scene. Usually, the result will look fine. Sometimes, however, a particular part of a scene is more important to you than the rest. The camera cannot deduce this, and in settling for an average exposure it may over- or underexpose the key area of your composition. That is where your creative choice comes in. This section not only explains how to determine the exposure you want, but looks at different types of light, the effects they can create in a picture, and the extent to which you can control them.

Sun behind the subject *makes exposure hard to judge. The camera's meter is bound to read the bright sky and indicate an exposure setting that will cut down the light. In such situations you have to override the meter – as the photographer did here. The amount of light is just right for the three figures, although the meter needle indicates overexposure. With less light, they would have appeared only as silhouettes.*

Controlling light

The light reflected from the world around us varies enormously in intensity. On a sunny day, the scene may be several hundred times as bright outdoors as indoors. Our eyes quickly adjust to these different levels of brightness, but film is not as versatile – it needs a precisely fixed amount of light to form a good image. To get correctly exposed pictures you have to control the light that enters the camera, by first measuring the brightness of the scene and then adjusting your aperture and shutter speed until the quantity of light hitting the film exactly matches the film's sensitivity.

Both shutter and aperture halve or double the amount of light reaching the film each time you adjust their control scales by one full step. Thus, controlling the light is a simple matter of increasing or decreasing either the shutter speed or the size of the aperture. If you balance an increase of shutter speed against a decrease of aperture (or vice versa) the total amount of light reaching the film remains constant. As the diagrams below make clear, several different combinations of aperture and shutter speed can give you the same effective exposure.

This is not to say that each combination will produce the same image. In the picture of wine flowing into a glass at bottom left, a fast shutter freezes the movement, but a wide aperture throws the background out of focus. Conversely, as the shutter speed slows and the aperture narrows, the decanter in the background comes into focus but the flowing liquid blurs. Varying the aperture and shutter speed thus gives you creative control over the picture.

In very bright light, there may be a wide range of possible shutter and aperture combinations. But in dim light your choice will be more restricted. The photographer of the mother and child at the foot of the opposite page, for example, could not use too slow a shutter without blurring the picture, and had to choose the widest possible aperture to deliver enough light to the film.

Aperture and shutter speed
These two controls determine exposure in much the same way as length and diameter affect volume: though the disc representing light on the left is short and fat, it has exactly the same volume as the long, thin stick of light on the right – a long exposure at a small aperture.

Think of exposure as an hourglass – just as the same amount of sand runs more quickly through the hourglass on the left, so doubling the aperture lets through the same amount of light in half the time.

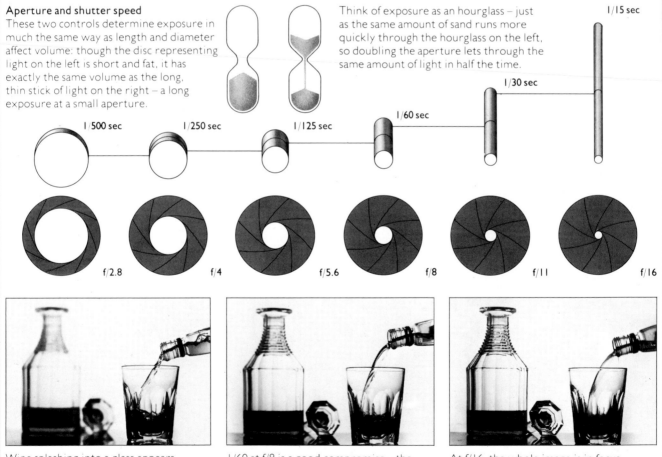

1/500 sec   1/250 sec   1/125 sec   1/60 sec   1/30 sec   1/15 sec

f/2.8   f/4   f/5.6   f/8   f/11   f/16

Wine splashing into a glass appears motionless at 1/500, but the brief exposure forces the use of a wide aperture, so there is little depth of field.

1/60 at f/8 is a good compromise – the film gets the same exposure, and the decanter is sharper, although the wine now shows signs of movement.

At f/16, the whole image is in focus, but getting correct exposure at this small aperture means using a speed of 1/15 – so the pouring wine is blurred.

Summer shadows cut a bold pattern of lines on the road, and draw your eye toward the car in the middle distance. The bright light gave the photographer plenty of freedom to choose shutter speed and aperture, so it was possible to keep the picture sharp from foreground to background by using a shutter speed of 1/250 and an aperture of f/11.

At a firework display there are far fewer choices – here the photographer needed a shutter speed of 1/125 to keep the group sharp, so he set the lens to its widest aperture to make the most of the dim light. He had to forgo depth of field.

Measuring light

Most modern cameras have some form of built-in light metering system that measures the brightness of the scene by means of light-sensitive cells, relates this to the film speed you have set, and either makes or recommends an appropriate exposure setting. When you point the camera at a subject and trigger the meter, you may see a viewfinder display of the shutter speed or aperture – or both – that the camera has set. Simpler automatic cameras generally warn you only if there is a risk of over- or underexposure. And on cameras with manual metering, a needle, or a digital display, indicates how you should change the camera's controls to get the right exposure. Most SLRs have through-the-lens (TTL) metering: cells inside the camera which read the brightness of the light after it has passed through the lens.

Meters indicate "correct" exposure as one that will record the subject in a mid-tone, between light and dark. The intention is to provide maximum detail, and an exposure suitable for most subjects. As a result, if you aim the camera at a sunlit wall the meter will select an exposure that will show the wall mid-gray in tone. If you point it at the same wall in deep shadow, the meter will recommend more exposure – again trying to show the wall mid-gray. Normally, however, in a scene of sun and shadow, the highlights are almost white, shady areas are dark and only some areas are mid-gray. Meters vary in the way they cope with this. They may simply average out the brightness of the whole image, but often they weight the average toward areas of the frame that are usually most important in pictures – the center and lower half. Some allow "spot metering," taking the reading from a small central area of the viewfinder, giving that the most detail.

The secret of successful exposure decisions is to understand how your particular meter reads a scene and to visualize in advance how you want the picture to look. No matter how sophisticated your camera, you alone can make the creative decisions.

Light-sensitive cells

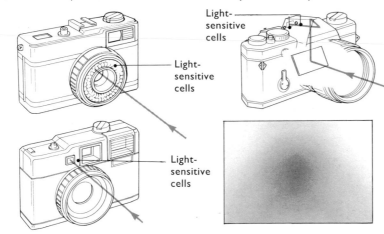

Light-sensitive cells

Light-sensitive cells

Light-sensitive cells

Through-the-lens metering (left)
Most SLR cameras have cells that measure the brightness of the light entering the camera through the lens. This provides a more accurate estimate of correct exposure than external metering.

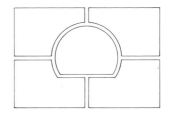

External metering (above)
Simple cameras incorporate the light-sensitive cells of the metering system either on the lens or in a window on the body to read reflected light.

Center-weighted metering (above)
Many SLRs measure the light reflected from the whole subject, but give extra emphasis to the brightness of the central area.

Intelligent metering (above)
Some cameras meter from several areas of the frame, comparing the readings with stored brightness patterns of typical photo subjects.

Handheld meters

Handheld incident meters give very accurate readings, as they measure the light falling onto a subject, rather than the reflected light. This means that the reading is not influenced by the subject's tones – under even lighting, dark, light and mid tones are all recorded faithfully. To take a reading, the meter is held in front of the subject, pointing at the camera. The meter then displays the recommended aperture and shutter speed settings.

Understanding your meter
A center-weighted meter gave perfect exposure for the skin tones opposite right, because the subject's face and arms filled the area of the frame given priority in this type of meter's system of averaging light. With a meter that measures light equally over the whole scene. This kind of shot is harder to get right. The bright sky behind the subject may influence the meter to indicate less exposure than the main subject needs. To avoid making errors you must know your own meter.

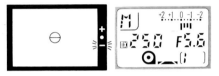

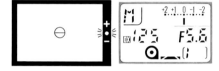

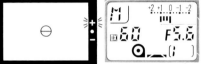

Underexposure
When the minus sign glows, or the bar pattern on the LCD shows a negative value, your pictures will be dark.

Correct exposure
When the zero in the viewfinder glows, or the LCD shows "0", your pictures will be correctly exposed.

Overexposure
When the plus sign glows, or the bar pattern on the LCD shows a positive value, your pictures will be too light.

Manual or automatic/1

All but the most basic new cameras have some method of automatic exposure control, and many have a wide choice of exposure modes. The quickest and simplest way of setting shutter speed and aperture is programmed exposure mode. If it is set to "program", the camera automatically chooses an appropriate combination of shutter speed and aperture according to the film speed and the brightness of the light reflected by the subject. In the dimmest conditions, the camera sets the lens to its maximum aperture and chooses the slowest shutter speed available. With progressively brighter subjects, the program sets faster and faster shutter speeds until it is able to set a shutter speed that will eliminate the effects of camera-shake (usually 1/60 or 1/125). The program then sets a combination of faster shutter speeds and smaller apertures as the light gets brighter.

Some programmed exposure modes take into consideration the focal length of the lens. When a telephoto lens is fitted to the camera, the program sets faster shutter speeds as there is a greater risk of camera-shake. With a short focal length lens, the risk of camera-shake is less, so instead of setting fast shutter speeds the program sets narrow apertures, which give greater depth of field.

The main drawback of programmed exposure is that the camera assumes complete control over the exposure settings. However, some cameras feature "program shift", which can be used to alter the exposure settings chosen by the camera.

Many cameras have advanced programmed exposure modes that are designed for particular types of photography. For example, speed programs (often known as sports programs) favor fast shutter speeds and choose smaller apertures only when the top shutter speed has been set. On some modern autofocus cameras, the speed program automatically selects continuous focus mode.

Semi-automatic exposure gives the photographer more control than programmed exposure, but is still quick to use. There are two modes: shutter priority and aperture priority. In shutter priority mode, the photographer chooses a shutter speed and the camera selects an appropriate aperture. Conversely, in aperture priority mode, the photographer selects an aperture setting and the camera sets an appropriate shutter speed.

Manual exposure provides maximum control, because the photographer sets both shutter speed and aperture, but it is the slowest exposure mode to use. A display in the viewfinder – and on the LCD panel, if the camera has one – shows that the selected combination of settings will give a correct exposure, or indicates how to alter the settings to get the exposure right.

Programmed exposure

In program mode the camera measures the subject brightness and the program sets an appropriate aperture and shutter speed combination, based on the focal length of the lens and the film speed. As the light level changes, the program automatically adjusts the exposure settings to maintain

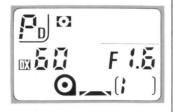

a correct exposure. It may also select the autofocus. Program modes are ideal for candid photography.

Semi-automatic exposure

The two semi-automatic exposure modes give the photographer more creative control over exposure. In shutter priority mode, as right, you set the shutter speed and the camera sets the aperture, giving you control over the sharpness of the image. In aperture priority mode you set the

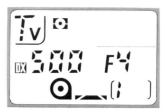

aperture and the camera selects an appropriate shutter speed, giving you control over depth of field.

Manual exposure

Manual exposure is slow to use but offers the most control. You can experiment with a wide range of aperture and shutter speed combinations for different effects.

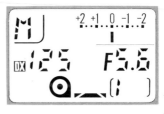

Creative control is needed with some subjects. Using a manual camera, the photographer could set the controls to overexpose the pavement and stop the little boy appearing as a silhouette.

Depth of field is important in the tranquil park scene above. The photographer wanted to show everything in sharp detail from the dappled foreground to the distant background figures. Aperture priority exposure mode, or a depth program, suits this type of scene.

Movement and timing are the crucial elements of the shot on the left. A fast shutter speed, and a quick response, have caught the flying spray and sense of fun perfectly. A shutter priority mode enabled the photographer to set the speed and then concentrate on the action.

Manual and automatic/2

When can you trust your camera meter, and when should you override it? If scenes with an average distribution of tones are lit from the front or the side, the camera's meter will probably serve well enough. But if the light is coming from behind the subject, for example, the meter may give a reading for the bright background so that the subject itself is underexposed and appears as a silhouette. Exposure often involves a creative decision and the meter's reading should be seen as a starting point. Identify the part of the scene you consider the main subject of the picture. If this is much lighter or darker than the rest, you should adjust the exposure to show good detail there, rather than accepting an average of the whole scene.

An effective way of basing exposure on the most important area is to take a "key reading" close to the main subject before moving back to your shooting position. You can do this readily with manual exposure controls but need some other method with automatic systems, such as a memory lock, which allows you to set the exposure and then hold it while you move to another camera position. Alternatively, you can use a compensation control, which allows you to choose several stops more or less exposure than the meter suggested.

Mixed light and dark areas in the same shot require care. If you think a light background such as the sky is biasing the meter, compensate by giving one or two stops extra exposure. Conversely, if you have a small, light subject against a dark background, give slightly less exposure than is indicated. For scenes with important detail in both light and dark areas, take readings for each and pick the midway setting.

When you are in doubt, "bracketing" offers a solution. Take the same shot three or five times, changing the exposure in either third- or half-stop increments around the setting you think is correct. Cameras with an autobracketing function can do this for you. When you press the shutter release, the camera takes a series of shots (usually three), at, above, and below the exposure reading.

Exposure compensation
Automatic cameras often have an exposure control. A light subject (right) may appear dull at the automatic exposure, but plus one stop on the control restores the true brightness (far right).

Reading from a face

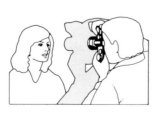

1 – When you need to set the exposure for an important element such as a face, move close so that the face fills the whole frame, and set the exposure.

2 – Then move back to your chosen camera position and take the shot at the same setting. Some automatic cameras have a memory lock to help you do this.

Bracketing is advisable when you are unsure of a reading. The meter alone could not determine the right balance in the scene below. The photographer made five varying exposures and selected the third frame as the best for enlargement.

The exposure you want

Despite all the sophistication of through-the-lens meters, accurate exposure is still technically the most difficult part of photography. Because film can reproduce only a part of the enormous brightness range the eye sees on a sunny day, exposure meters can suggest a setting suitable only for an average of the main tones in the picture. They take no account of the photographer's wish to show clearly all the details in a particular shadow or highlight area.

A useful way to look at a scene is to imagine that a bright sunlit view contains ten main levels of brightness. (One such view is diagrammed at the top of the opposite page.) Different films vary in the brightness range they can handle, but in practice you can assume that the image on the film will show good detail in only five or six of these levels. Parts of the scene beyond these limits will show as entirely dark or light, with no visible detail. Therefore, with high-contrast subjects, you have to decide which parts of the scene you consider most important and adjust the exposure to make sure that they fall within the range of the film. This is a creative decision, and the examples on these two pages show that you often have to sacrifice some of what the eye can see. If the most important detail is in a portion of the subject that is significantly brighter than the rest of the scene, give one or two stops less exposure than that indicated by the average reading, to avoid overexposing this detail. Conversely, if the important detail is in a dark part of a predominantly light scene, increase the metered exposure by one or two stops.

Sunlight streaming through a window creates a brightness range too great for the film. Setting exposure for the light area records detail only in the garden.

Giving two stops extra exposure shows the foreground detail fully, but the highlights around the window are burned out, unbalancing the composition.

The tonal range of the scene
(above) covers nine out of a
possible ten brightness levels –
represented diagrammatically
by the spots. Because only six
of these levels will show good,
clear detail on the film, the
photographer must select the
most important area.

A simplified tonal range
divides the scene into three
main areas: first, the bright
garden, then a well lit middle
portion and finally the darkest
parts of the foreground. This
foreground clearly needs some
extra exposure for the picture
to have visual interest.

With one stop more exposure than
the averaged meter reading, the detail
in the garden vanishes but the strongest
areas of interest show up well.

Into the light

Keeping the light source behind the camera almost always guarantees a clear, detailed image. However, to realize the full potential of different subjects, you need to accept the challenge of taking pictures in less conventional lighting conditions. Several of the pictures on these two pages show how you can bring sparkle to otherwise ordinary scenes by photographing into the light.

Backlighting always accentuates shape. A solid object with the sun directly behind will be reduced to a black outline. But if the subject lets some light through, the effect will be quite different. In the picture of the ruined abbey at left below, pale sunlight passing through small gaps between the stones casts a radiating pattern on the grass, yet the contrast is low enough for an exposure that also shows clearly the texture of the shadowed walls. With transparent and translucent subjects, backlighting can often intensify colors and reveal hidden structures. For example, in the photograph at the bottom of this page, the rimlit red and yellow leaves at the ends of the branches glow with color, while shadows within the lacy pattern of green leaves show the complex structure of the branches.

In strongly backlit scenes, the contrast between bright highlights and dark shadows needs to be taken into account when calculating exposure. As a general rule, if you want to record shadow details clearly, you should take a close-up reading from the most important area.

Coppery backlighting burnishes the leaves of a plant. The photographer shone a reading lamp on the wall behind the plant and took the picture on daylight film, using a No. 10 red filter to intensify the warm color of the tungsten light. Room lighting reveals some of the decorative detail on the pot.

Low sun streaming through a narrow arched window is the dazzling focal point for the image of an ancient abbey, above. Shadows cast by the acutely angled rays create perspective lines that lead the viewer into the picture and convey a sense of depth.

Strong light directly behind a spreading tree picks out shapes, patterns and colors against the dark background. The contrast between bright highlights, on the outermost leaves, and solid shadows, where branches and foliage block the light, adds to the impact of the composition.

106

A fine spray striking a surfer disperses the sun's rays into thousands of tiny particles, stippling the whole scene with sparkling light. With plenty of reflected light in the shadow areas, the photographer based exposure on an average reading.

Raking light

Many photographers are wary of taking photographs in bright sun because of the problems of high contrast. But at the right time of day, clear sunlight offers marvelous photographic opportunities.

In midmorning, and again in the afternoon and early evening, the low sun sends oblique shafts of light across a scene, picking out textural details that are lost in flatter lighting. As the position of the sun moves more to the side of the subject, shadows become larger and longer. Yet because the light is less intense than at midday, these shadows are soft-edged rather than harsh. This sets up a subtle play of light and shade often exploited by landscape photographers to give modeling and depth, as in the pastoral scene opposite. You can use the same lighting effect to give drama and atmosphere to any subject. Viewed from the side, a figure facing a low-angled sun will be outlined with a golden light that appears both warm and flattering. The profiled girl at far right is an example.

Going out with a camera and observing how the colors, forms and moods of a scene change according to the sun's position is by far the best way to discover lighting effects. Sometimes, returning to your subject an hour later can make a surprising difference. But you do not always have to wait for the sun to move. To get the striking picture at the bottom of this page, the photographer changed his viewpoint by walking around the corner of the block and took the second picture with the slanting sunlight falling across the subject.

Moving the camera
Altering the direction of the light resulted in two very different images of the same subject (right). Harsh frontal lighting registered the old man, the plants and the wrought-iron balcony in equally sharp detail (1). By walking around the corner, the photographer got a far more atmospheric view (2). Bright sunlight from one side casts a halo around the man's white hair and transforms the ornate metalwork into glittering silver filigree.

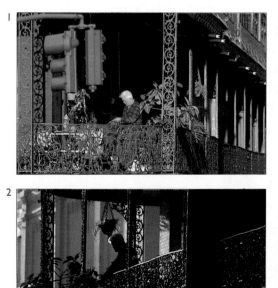

Low evening sun rakes across a hilly landscape dotted with sheep. The lengthy shadows cast at this time on a bright day, together with the warmth and clarity of the light, are perfect for bringing out form and texture in such scenes. Here, sunlight catching the poplars makes an interesting contrast with the dark line of firs standing high on the horizon.

Oblique rays from late afternoon sun skate over a craggy rock and gently gild the profile of a girl gazing out to sea. Light reflected off the sand and water creates a hazy background that adds to the strong romantic mood of the picture.

109

Sunlight controlled

Strong sunshine tends to produce such extreme contrast that deep shadows or blank highlights may spoil your pictures, regardless of how well you judge the exposure. But you can radically improve photographs by using simple techniques to modify the light falling on a subject – especially if the subject is of a manageable size.

The simplest way to reduce high contrast is to move the subject into the shade. If you are photographing people in a landscape setting, the shade of a tree will provide a much more even tone on their faces than if they stand in the open. Be careful to take the exposure reading close to the subject so that the meter is not influenced unduly by the bright sunshine beyond. Another technique is to reduce the intensity of the light by rigging up a diffuser between the sun and the subject. For example, if you shield a flower with a piece of translucent paper or a

sheet of thin white cloth, the highlights will be less bright and the shadows softer.

A more practical solution may be to fill-in the shadows with flash at reduced power. Advanced flash units control fill-in lighting automatically, but with more basic automatic units set the ISO rating on the flash at double that of the film in use. With a manual flash set the unit to half power or wrap a paper tissue over the front. For fill-in flash in bright, sunny conditions, a powerful flash unit is required.

You can also reduce contrast by reflecting natural light back into the shadows. A reflective surface, such as a white wall, acts as an excellent balancing light source. Alternatively, you can introduce special reflectors such as those shown below and in the diagrams on the opposite page – or simply use a hand mirror, carefully angled to reflect a beam of light into a specific area of shadow.

White clothes gleam brightly in the light from a flash unit in this outdoor fashion picture. The photographer set the exposure for the shaded building behind, then halved the flash power.

Special reflectors
You can use any bright, reflective surface to throw light into shadow areas, but portable reflectors are standard equipment for portrait and still-life photography. Several bought or home-made types are shown below. Umbrella reflectors can be folded for transport.

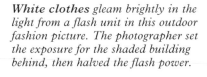

Folding silvered umbrella

Crumpled cooking foil on board

White card or polystyrene

Daylight from a window shines strongly on this informal still-life arrangement on a basketwork surface, as diagrammed above. The directional light shows up shape and texture well.

A large white card, placed in front of the subject and to the right, reflects some light back into the deep shadow on the hat, adding foreground detail.

A large mirror replacing the card fills the shadow completely. With the card moved to the left, the jug is lit as well, and the emphasis of the picture shifts to the bright foreground.

Handling limited light

Low light produces some of the most evocative and spectacular photographs you can take – from sunsets and dimly lit interiors to street scenes at night with illuminated signs and floodlit buildings. In order to use limited lighting effectively, you need first of all to escape from the idea that the only acceptable image is one that is evenly and brightly lit. At night or in a dark interior, for example, there is often too little light or too much contrast between highlights and shadows to obtain full detail over the whole image. Make a virtue of necessity, and take advantage of the way low light simplifies an image. You may be able to create a strong silhouette or take a shot in which the light forms an interesting rim around the subject. A good time to experiment is at dusk, when there is still enough light for a relatively short exposure, but street and house lights evoke a nocturnal mood.

To obtain enough light for exposure in low lighting situations, you often need to use both wide apertures and slow shutter speeds. You can shoot some subjects with a handheld camera if you have fast film and a lens with a wide maximum aperture – at least f/2.8. But many subjects demand a slow exposure, requiring a tripod or other form of camera support. When using a wide-angle or standard 50mm lens, support the camera for exposures slower than 1/60; with a long lens, 1/125 is about the slowest safe speed for handheld shots. One great advantage of a tripod and a long exposure is that you can use a very small aperture and so increase the overall sharpness of your image. However, very long exposures in dim light can produce unpredictable effects, especially with color film, so you may need to try several different exposures to get the picture right.

Low light exposure guide
Exposure readings tend to be misleading in low light, but you can use this chart for typical subjects as a rough guide.

FILM IN USE	ISO 100		ISO 400	
Brightly lit shop windows	1/30	f/2.8	1/60	f/4
Well-lit street scenes	1/30	f/2	1/60	f/2.8
Fireworks	1/8	f/2.8	1/30	f/4
Floodlit buildings	2 secs	f/5.6	1/2	f/5.6
Street lights	1/4	f/2	1/15	f/2
Neon signs	1/30	f/4	1/125	f/4
Dim church interior	10 secs	f/4	$2\frac{1}{2}$ secs	f/4
Landscape at full moon	20 secs	f/2.8	5 secs	f/2.8

Making a time exposure
For exposures longer than 1 sec, use the "B" or time setting. This keeps the shutter open for as long as the release is pressed. A tripod and cable release will prevent camera shake.

Other camera supports
You can keep the camera steady by resting it on a firm surface or by cushioning it with a beanbag.

Snaking streaks *of light (left) were created by a time exposure that recorded the head and tail lights of cars moving across the bridge. The evening sky provided the meter reading to show the bridge in silhouette.*

Delicate rimlighting *traces the monk's profile to produce a powerful portrait – the photographer metered the light on the monk's forehead, and gave one stop more exposure.*

Shimmering water *reflects light from the evening sun, backlighting the figures and foreground. To reduce the foreground to silhouettes, the photographer metered the bright area of water.*

Using flash

The most portable and convenient means of providing extra light for photography is an electronic flash unit. This fits onto an accessory slot – known as the hotshoe – on top of the camera. When you release the shutter, the flash unit discharges a brief, intense flash of light.

The duration of the flash – between 1/1000 and 1/50,000 – determines the length of the exposure. You need to adjust the shutter speed only to ensure that when the flash fires the entire frame is exposed. This means setting the camera's flash synchronization speed or a slower speed.

There are three categories of flash unit: manual, self-regulating and dedicated TTL. Manual units are the most basic – they discharge the same brightness of light on every flash, leaving you to control the exposure using the aperture settings on the lens. An exposure chart indicates which aperture to use for different flash-to-subject distances and film speeds.

Self-regulating units offer a degree of automatic exposure control. A sensor cell measures the light reflected from a subject, and the unit quenches flash output automatically when the subject has received enough light. A chart or dial shows which aperture, or apertures, you can set.

Dedicated TTL units offer advanced features and are designed for use with particular cameras. They link up with a camera's through-the-lens (TTL) metering system to control exposure automatically.

Most compacts, and some SLRs, have a built-in flash unit. These units are low powered, but many have a range of advanced features.

Power control

Aperture choice indicator arrows

Aperture scale

Scale of maximum flash-to-subject distances

Film speed window

On-off switch

Ready light

Using a self-regulating flash
The on-camera flash unit above has a calculator dial (enlarged above right) on its top surface. As an example, the dial has been set to show which f-stops you may choose if you are using ISO 200 film. You have a choice of f/4 or f/8 – the white and black arrows point to these f-numbers, and the maximum working distances appear alongside. In the operating sequence explained at the right, you select the correct power output with a switch elsewhere on the unit – again marked in white and black to correspond with the chosen aperture.

1 – Turn the calculator dial until the speed of the film in use appears in the window.

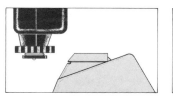

2 – Slide the foot of the flash unit into the camera's hot shoe.

3 – Set the shutter speed to the camera's flash synchronization speed.

4 – Gauge the distance to the subject. Then choose the f-stop – here f/4 for 20 feet.

5 – Slide power control to the setting that corresponds with the aperture chosen.

6 – Switch on flash unit. You can take pictures soon after the ready light glows.

Self-regulating flash (left)
Units such as the one at left give a choice of automatic aperture settings. The flash head can be tilted to bounce light off a ceiling.

Dedicated TTL flash
(below left)
The flash unit below links up with the electronics in particular cameras to give fully automatic exposure control. It calculates the duration of each flash by

analysing light readings from the camera's through-the-lens (TTL) metering system, and camera-to-subject distance information from special autofocus lenses. An automatic zoom head mechanism matches flash coverage to the field of view of the lens. The AF auxiliary light, positioned below the flash head, emits an infra-red beam in dim light to facilitate autofocusing.

Hammerhead flash
(below)
The powerful flash unit at right is attached to the camera by means of a bracket and a cord. The flash head can be tilted upwards to provide bounce flash.

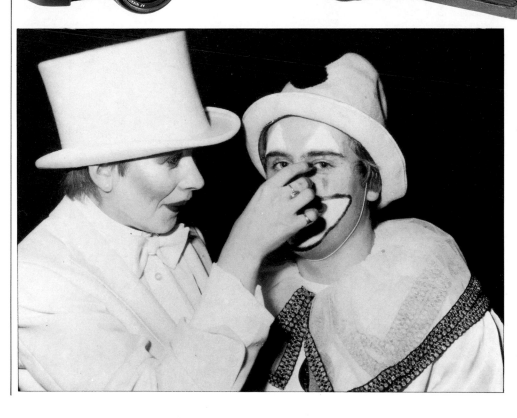

If you use flash to light a portrait subject, you may find that the subject's eyes appear bright red in your pictures. This is known as "red eye", and it is caused by light from the flash reflecting off the back of the subject's eyes and into the camera lens.

Some modern cameras with built-in flash units have a special pre-flash mode (also known as red eye reduction control). When pre-flash mode is activated, the flash fires several low strength bursts of light at the subject just before it fires. This makes the subject's pupils contract, which lessens the red eye effect.

Using simple filters

Sometimes you can improve your pictures by using filters to change, control, or partially block light entering the lens. Although this may sound complicated, filters are just thin sheets of glass, gelatin or plastic that either screw onto the lens front or slip into special holders in the same position.

The filters that are used most often are those that clean up the light from the subject. Skylight or ultraviolet (UV) filters absorb ultraviolet radiation, which can make distant objects appear hazy, particularly when conditions are very bright. Use them in conjunction with a lens hood, which will help to exclude the stray light that sometimes reaches the lens, causing flare and softening the image.

In some circumstances, a polarizing filter can produce even more useful effects. This filter can cut down glare from the sky, from water, from glass or other non-metallic reflective surfaces. Light traveling from these surfaces often becomes polarized, which means that it vibrates mainly in one plane instead of at all angles perpendicular to its line of direction. By blocking the polarized plane, the filter gives a more clearly defined image, and will attractively darken a blue sky.

Another important group of filters absorbs specific colors. A pale yellow filter, for example, passes red and green light but blocks blue. Because this leaves the blue areas underexposed, yellow filters can be used in black-and-white photography to darken the sky and make clouds stand out boldly. With color film, however, every part of the scene will be subtly tinted toward the color of the filter you use. The yellowish series of filters widely known by the Kodak serial number 81, for example, can be used to impart a general warm tint.

You can also buy a great variety of special effects filters. Use them with care as they can all too easily create effects that are garish rather than attractive.

No filter

With polarizing filter

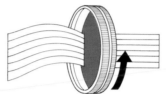

Polarizing filter
This type of filter helps to cut unwanted glare. Rotate the filter's ring until the image in the viewfinder darkens.

The startling difference between the two pictures of prehistoric rock engravings in Utah (above) shows the ability of a polarizing filter to reveal detail that would otherwise be hidden by glare. Polarizing filters also have the effect of darkening blue skies, as in the atmospheric picture of trees (below), and can often enliven landscapes.

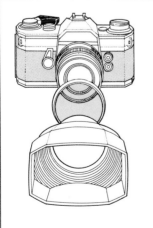

UV filter and lens hood
An ultraviolet filter attached permanently to the lens will improve your outdoor pictures and protect the delicate front of the lens. Lens hoods should frame the picture area closely. Square types such as the one at left with modified corners do this most effectively. They are particularly suited to wide-angle lenses, because circular hoods sometimes cut off the corners of the image at wide apertures.

A soft, misty look can be introduced with a diffusion filter as in the romantic image of the flowers in the picture at far right.

The seascape below has been improved by a graduated filter that darkens part of the image. Without the filter, the sky would have appeared as an empty area of white. The filter contributes the color.

USING COLOR CREATIVELY

Color does more than bring photographs closer to reality. Particular colors often provoke strong responses in the viewer, creating tension or excitement, establishing a soothing feeling of equilibrium or jarring the senses. These powerful reactions may be independent of the subject of the picture, for we react to color emotionally.

Controlling the strength or placement of colors can enable you to produce more effective color pictures. On a few occasions you will have the opportunity to alter the colors of the subject – you could, for example, ask someone to wear a particular color, or change the color of a backdrop. Much more easily, you can manipulate the colors that actually appear in the image by using techniques of composition outlined in this section. For example, you can choose a viewpoint or a lens to include certain areas of color and exclude others. You can fill the viewfinder frame with vivid hues or restrict bright color to just a small area. And you can juxtapose colors for a calming or a vigorous effect.

Understanding the relationship between color and light will further help you to exploit the full potential of the scene you are photographing. This means that time of day and weather strongly influence your pictures, as does whether you are photographing in natural or artificial light.

Colors create mood – that is part of their magic. By using them in a controlled way, you can give pictures just the impact or subtlety you want.

A rainbow in the spray from a fire hose reveals the colors of the sunlight flooding a Pittsburgh intersection. By having the colors arc over the policeman, the photographer infused an ordinary street scene with a sense of wonder.

The richness of color

Strong colors have a more direct impact than those that are muted. Of course, many good photographs have soft colors, for these subtler hues often contribute to the sense of balance or atmosphere in a shot. But when you want colors to contribute drama or have a vigorous effect, you usually want them to appear at their most vivid.

The strongest colors are said to be fully "saturated" – a term borrowed from the dyeing industry. In photography, saturated colors are those that consist of one or two of the primary colors of light – red, green or blue – but not all three, because that introduces an element of grayness. At the same time the saturated colors look most vivid in a certain kind of lighting. For example, a pure red flower will appear more vivid than one that has a brownish tinge, but both will appear most colorful in bright, diffused light. Direct sunlight can make a color

appear less vivid by lightening it – as the left-hand picture of the leaves below demonstrates. Shade, on the other hand, can make the colors appear darker.

When you have identified an area of color that you want to emphasize, the following techniques may help you take full advantage of its richness. First, consider whether you can move around until the angle at which light strikes the subject brings out the strongest color. Unless the subject reflects glare, a position with the sun behind the camera will usually be best. Second, to reproduce the color at maximum saturation, take the exposure reading from the chosen part of the scene rather than the whole view. Although this may underexpose duller parts of the subject, the contrast can enhance the chosen color area. Finally, with some slide films, deliberately underexposing by a half-stop can enrich color, as well as producing good highlight detail.

*1 – **Glare** reflecting from a shiny bush (above) gives the entire photograph a washed-out appearance. The other two pictures were taken in the same light, showing that color saturation in direct sunlight depends on the lighting angle.*

*2 – **Backlighting**, with the bush between camera and sun, gives dramatic contrast in which the leaves are very bright. But because the light shining through the leaves is too harsh, the colors appear somewhat washed-out.*

*3 – **Bright light without glare** shows fully saturated leaves. The photographer took up a position different from the first two, altering the angle between sun, subject and camera. Slight underexposure increases the richly colored effect.*

Color saturation
Pure colors lose intensity if they are either darkened or lightened. The saturated hues at the center of the diagram are progressively desaturated by the addition of white or black. In photography, this means that colors lose strength in shade, or as light glares from a surface. Exposure errors also make colors look less vivid.

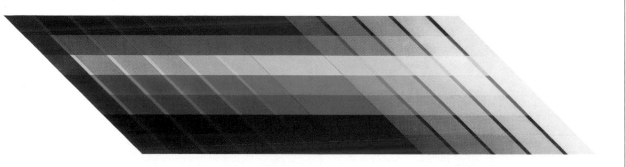

Low light mutes even the pure colors of these flowering trees, an effect that is increased by the haze. The green foliage is so dulled that it is almost gray in color. In conditions such as these, only the strongest colors, perfectly exposed, will preserve any intensity.

Perfectly lit by soft window light, a bowl of fruit shows the richness of fully saturated colors. But even here, the effect of light reflecting from the subject can be seen in the highlights on the green apples. With slightly more exposure, these areas would have begun to appear too light and washed-out.

The dominant color

The ability of modern color film to reproduce all the brilliant colors around us tempts photographers to fill the viewing frame with the richest mixture possible. Sheer profusion of color sometimes works well, but if you are not careful, the picture becomes a jumble of clashing hues.

Often, you can exploit rich, bright color more simply by allowing just one powerful hue to dominate the image. Restricting the color palette in this way can concentrate the impact of the picture – in the startlingly blue seascape shown below, the single block of color seems more emphatic than would several colors jostling for attention.

This way of using color often works best when the dominant color forms a unified background – as does the bright yellow of the umbrella on the right. The more intense the color, the more it will dominate the image, but paler color areas can be used to frame areas of the photograph that are a different hue. For example, in the picture on the right, the lemon of the umbrella makes a lively and vivid backdrop for the girl's shy smile.

To make best use of large, commanding areas of color, try to set them off against other, more neutral, parts of the picture – here the black of the girl's hair, and her white shirt. You may be able to compose the picture so as to exclude discordant, distracting colors in favor of muted hues, such as the soft browns of earth – or of skin itself.

Sea and sky turn deep azure in dawn light.
The dark color, deliberately underexposed,
emphasizes the lights of the island temple.

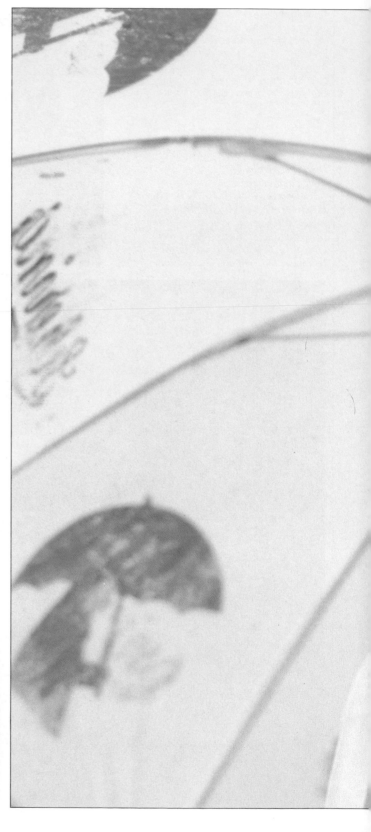

*A yellow **umbrella** makes a vibrant background for this simple picture – a delightful rainy-day portrait. The light filtering through the fabric is soft and flattering, warming the whole image, and enhancing the tones of the girl's skin.*

Limited color

Images that have very little color at all can some-times be extraordinarily evocative. Such nearly monochromatic pictures are expressive in a much more subtle way than are most color photographs, but they often have a compelling simplicity and beauty. Not least, they draw our attention because they are relatively uncommon.

Two main types of monochromatic images are those in which the lighting or the prevailing weather conditions provide an overall draining or blending of colors, and those in which the subject itself has little variety of color. A landscape lit by weak sun early or late in the day, will tend to have a predominant orange glow, especially if there is a haze or dust in the air. Rain, fog, mist, smoke – even pollution in industrial areas – scatter light and mute colors, reducing the color range of the most variegated subjects. You can sometimes use the glow of a fire or the color of artificial light to tint a scene with a single, overall color. One useful tip for enhancing the effect of a colored light source is to shoot toward it without a lens shade, so that light flaring into the lens spreads the color over the whole image, often producing attractive effects.

Subjects that are monochromatic in themselves are usually more difficult to find – unless you can take the picture at close range. As a general rule, the larger your subject, the more likely it is to contain a variety of colors. For this reason, a long lens with its narrow field of view is far more useful than is a wide-angle lens for limiting the color range. Finally, you can always underline the prevailing mood of an existing color range with a pale colored filter.

Soft spray, thrown up by the turbulent waters of Victoria Falls, scatters the light, suppressing true colors and rendering the whole scene in a subdued sepia tone. Only the skeleton of the tree stands out against the mist.

White and black tones can make subtle, effective combinations on color film. You need to develop your powers of observation to find a picture as simple yet expressive as this one.

The golden sunset sky
suffuses the Cape of Good
Hope with glowing light.
A long lens has compressed
distance, bringing closer
the silhouetted ships on
the horizon.

Ice-blue tones of the grass
form a soft backdrop to the
dark shape of the horse,
photographed in failing
light. When using a limited
color range, look for bold
shapes to provide contrast.

Color harmony

Although the way we see colors is highly subjective, most people agree that certain combinations of colors appear more pleasing or harmonious to the eye than others. Moreover, a restricted range of colors makes it easier to create a harmonious composition. A photograph made up of slight variations of a single color, for example, will obviously convey a sense of harmony. So will a mixture of one main color with various neutral shades – grays, browns, white or black. Combining two or more colors requires care. As the color wheel on the right shows, adjacent hues harmonize readily, but opposites contrast strongly. Thus, blues merge well with greens, whereas red and green compete for the viewer's attention setting up an optical impression of vibrancy.

However, there are exceptions to the general rule. Colors that are adjacent on the wheel may clash if they are very bright – a vivid red combined with a bright magenta, for example. Conversely, strongly contrasting colors can harmonize if their tones are either dark and muted or pale and washed out. For example, in the picture of the beach huts on the opposite page, subdued light has blended together a number of different colors. Think of the way the muted red and golden hues of an autumn landscape blend with the subdued greens. In practice, photographing colors harmoniously is a matter of composing your shots carefully to exclude any colors you judge may detract from the mood of the whole. If the hues appear too strident, you can also try waiting for softer lighting from a low or diffused sun to tone everything down.

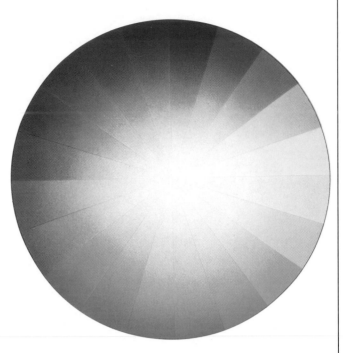

Color wheel
Arrangement of the main color components of light on a wheel makes it easy to see how different hues work together. Here, the wheel is made up of the three primary colors – red, green and blue – and their complementaries – cyan, magenta and yellow. Half the circle has "cool" colors – green, cyan and blue – and half has "warm" colors – magenta, red and yellow. Colors that are close together on the wheel harmonize. But if tones are made paler, even the most contrasting colors blend – as can be seen here toward the center of the wheel.

Bright orange berries vary the mosaic of green leaves, but they do not detract from the natural harmony of the yellow and greens. You can include a contrasting color without disturbing the balance of the whole, if the contrasting area is small enough. Here the photographer stresses patterns of color as the subject of the picture.

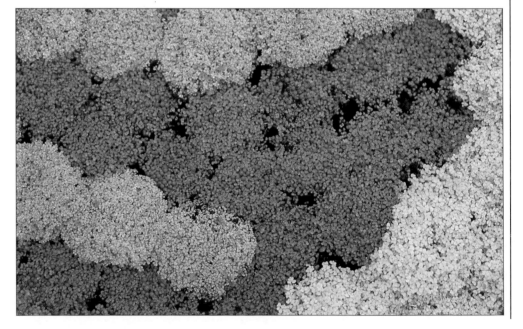

A row of beach huts at dusk creates a darkly harmonious color composition. In spite of the fairly wide range of colors, the tones are all muted and therefore convey a sense of tranquillity. The cool blue sand in the foreground helps to unify the shot.

Half a lemon, dried out by the sun, rests on a translucent painted plate. Although the lighting is bright and direct, all three of the colors blend together, providing a simple, but unusual example of warm color harmony.

Dramatic color

Just as some colors look balanced or harmonious when photographed together, others seem to contrast dramatically, and produce a bold, vibrant effect. You can use such dynamic combinations to inject excitement into a picture, to draw attention to a subject, or purely to create a strong abstract impact. Color contrast is most striking when you restrict your picture to two or three colors – any more than this and the effect will be restless.

The colors likely to produce the most striking contrast are those that lie opposite one another on the color wheel – the warm reds, yellows and oranges against the cool blues and greens, as in the photographs here. But what really determines how much two colors contrast is their relative brightness. Generally the effect is most dramatic if the two hues are equally bright. Pure color contrasts are often easier to find on a relatively small scale – by closing in on a shop window display, for example. When you have complete control over the ingredients of your picture, you can consciously set up bold color contrasts, as the photographer did for the fashion shot on the opposite page.

Ornamental plants often have colors almost as vivid as the artificial dyes and pigments in fabric and paint. At left, richly colored coleus leaves provide a perfect color contrast – red and green are opposite each other on the color wheel.

A delicate green sapling stands out crisply against the bright red fence, below left. The tree's fragility seems underlined by the strength of the red. A powerful yet very simple composition accentuates the dramatic contrast of colors.

A bright blue door makes the girl's yellow trousers look all the more vivid. The photographer has used the blue background to both isolate and frame the figure. And the picture shows how contrast increases when two light hues are juxtaposed.

129

Abstract color

You can give your pictures a striking abstract quality quite easily by exploiting bold color areas. All you need to do is to frame the subject so that colors rather than recognizable forms are emphasized.

A good way of making color abstract is to exclude part of the subject. We identify things largely by their outlines and the context in which we find them. Isolated by tight or unconventional framing, objects appear as a two-dimensional arrangement in the picture. The effect of the yellow dress opposite was achieved in this way. By cropping out the girl's head with the frame, the photographer has removed the obvious center of attention and concentrated on the composition as an arrangement of colors.

Alternatively, you can tilt the camera so that the subject, seen from an unusual angle, becomes less important than the colors. You can even try taking the picture with the subject deliberately out of focus to make the shapes less distinct and more to be enjoyed as areas of color.

Lighting is an important factor in emphasizing color at the expense of literal representation. Flat light on an overcast day can be used to give a two-dimensional effect because there are no shadows to throw objects into relief. On the other hand, direct sunlight, provided there is no glare, can illuminate colors and bring out strong contrasts between them, producing strikingly vivid effects.

An inflatable play space provides the setting for a boldly abstract composition. The photographer framed the scene to balance the three strong colors of the translucent material and has excluded any details that could act as reference points to help interpret the subject.

A short yellow dress and tanned legs contrast effectively with the deep-blue background. Judicious framing cuts out recognizable features of the human subject, transforming a fashion picture into an unusual abstract image.

Saturated color

You need to expose very carefully to bring out the brilliance of colors in direct sunlight, and to prevent them from becoming dissipated in glare and bouncing reflections. The pictures here show that colors often look richer in more diffused light. This is largely because contrast is reduced, making exposure easier to control. At the same time, the softer light helps to harmonize or balance colors – if that is your aim. And most important of all, diffused sunlight casts softer, less noticeable shadows. In portraiture, particularly, skin tones are thus recorded more accurately, and the whole image is less likely to be confused by the presence of deep, hard-edged shadows.

Light clouds and haze high in the sky diffuse light by redistributing the strongly directional rays of the sun across a larger part of the sky. The result is that shadows become less intense and their edges less sharp. Instead of being bright in the sun or dark in the shade, colors are brought closer together in tone. Provided the cloud cover is light, hues will retain their intensity. And, in the absence of hard shadows or reflected glare, the individual richness of the colors may actually increase. Because the key to showing any color at full saturation is accurate exposure, the reduced contrast between naturally dark and light colors will allow you to choose an exposure that suits both. The varied greens of landscapes can thus be recorded with equal brilliance in the muted light. And in portraits, you can more easily blend and balance flesh tones, clothing and background colors.

A red fish, photographed in Kenya, glows with an almost unnatural brilliance against the equally vivid colors of the fisherman's shorts and T-shirt. The hazy sun reveals the full saturation of all the colors, without the intrusion of dark shadows. And the light keeps to a minimum the glare from the shiny scales.

Soft skin colors gave the key reading for this picture. But the sunlight, diffused by light clouds, restricted the range of tones. Thus reds and greens are correctly exposed also, and appear fully saturated. This light is ideal when you want to bring out the soft modeling of a face.

A sea of tulips vibrates with color, every leaf, stalk and petal standing out in the soft light. Stronger sun might have made the flower heads gleam even more brightly, but the shadows created would have obscured the green parts of the plants, making them dark and underexposed on the film.

Muted color

Photographs in dense haze, mist or fog produce some of the most delicate and subtle color effects. These conditions not only weaken sunlight, but also spread the light around the subject, and themselves become part of the landscape. Haze is made up of microscopic particles suspended in the air — common during long, hot spells and also in polluted areas such as cities. The droplets of water that constitute mist and fog are larger and more often found at higher altitudes, or near rivers, lakes, or the sea.

Haze, mist and fog all thicken the atmosphere, acting as a kind of continuous filter. The result is that intense hues are muted to pastel. At the same time, colors tend to merge into a narrower range, creating images as beautiful and fragile as the harvesting scene below. In extremely dense mist or fog, the colors of a landscape may become almost monochromatic; hence the effects of these weather conditions can be useful if you want to give a soft overall tone to an image or to harmonize colors that would jar with each other in brighter, more direct light. And the absence of distracting detail can help you to appreciate the compositional qualities of a landscape more easily.

The softening of color in haze, mist or fog becomes more pronounced with distance. The farther the subject is from the camera, the more simplified and delicate the image becomes, so that in a misty landscape, the different parts of the scene often appear to be arranged in receding layers of lighter and lighter color, as in the picture of mountain ranges opposite. Sometimes, you can emphasize the sense of depth this produces by choosing a viewpoint that includes strong foreground colors.

Remember that the effect of fog and mist are not always regular and predictable. In a breeze, wisps of mist trail around trees, rocks and hillsides, often linking hues or emphasizing the colors of clear areas. And in dense but localized mist, of the kind that often hangs over wetlands early on a summer morning, trees and other subjects can appear almost in silhouette if the sun is directly behind them. Light itself then supplies the only color, and in low sun, the scene may appear in delicate tones of orange or pink. You should look out for such unusual effects and exploit them by experimenting with viewpoint and camera angle. They open up marvelous opportunities for mood and atmosphere.

Late afternoon haze makes
this Burmese agricultural
scene almost monochromatic,
turning everything a warm
golden color. The stubble
of the field enhances the
feeling of shimmering heat,
and the pale rim of light
around the group reveals a
perfect choice of exposure.

Receding mountains
are reduced here into broad
washes of color by early
morning mist. This creates
an imposing sense of depth
as the planes of color
fade from green to lighter
blues. The whole image is
given an ethereal quality
by the orange light tipping
the farthest ridges as the
sun penetrates the mist.

135

The balance of color/1

The sun, a candle and a glowing coal all give off light as they release heat. But the color of the light that each produces is not identical, because the heat at which each source burns varies enormously. As a result, each source sends out a different mixture of wavelengths, with substantial effects on the colors of the objects illuminated. These effects are particularly noticeable in color photographs because films are balanced to give accurate colors in light of a particular wavelength mixture.

There is no point in relying on your eyes to detect minor changes in lighting. We see what we expect to see, ignoring subtle variations of color. A white shirt will still look white to us whether we see it in sunlight or indoors under artificial light. However, film records the predominant color of the lighting literally. Ordinary film for daylight use is balanced for average noon light in which the illumination comes mainly from the predominantly white light of the direct sun. Unless you correct it with a filter, lighting of a very different balance will inevitably change the colors in photographs taken with this same film, producing unreal colors – an effect known as a color cast.

The color of a light source does not depend only on its heat. For example, atmospheric factors come into play when we consider the way daylight changes in color. As a result, whereas daylight or noon sun appears neutral, the wavelength mixture reaching us varies as the sun rises or sets. Similarly, clouds or haze filter out some wavelengths by absorption, or scatter others so that they predominate in the light reflected from the sky itself. On a clear day, the sky looks intensely blue because of the scattering of blue wavelengths by atmospheric molecules. And this means that the light is much bluer in shaded areas, where illumination comes only from the sky, than in areas reached by the light of direct sun.

Light sources can be codified according to their so-called color temperature on the kelvin (k) scale. Temperature is the mode of measurement because a heated object, such as an iron bar, will change color from red through yellow and white to dazzling blue as the temperature increases. But remember that the kelvin number assigned to a light source relates to the color of the light produced, not to the physical heat of the source. Thus, the color temperature of daylight may be higher (because bluer) on a cold overcast day when all the light is coming from the sky, than in direct warm sun. At midday, average (photographic) daylight has a color temperature of about 5,500k, and it is for light of this color temperature that most color films are balanced, giving accurate color in normal outdoor scenes.

The color temperature scale
Whether you are photographing in artificial or natural light, all light sources have a certain preponderance of wavelengths that give the lighting a particular color. These different colors are shown below as a band of rising color temperatures, extending from the reddish lighting characteristic of candlelight and sunsets up to the bluer light normally found in pictures taken in the shade or on overcast days. The color effects of natural light in various conditions are illustrated above the color temperature band, those of artificial light sources below the band.

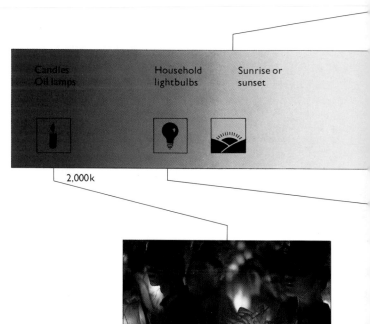

Candles
Oil lamps

Household lightbulbs

Sunrise or sunset

2,000k

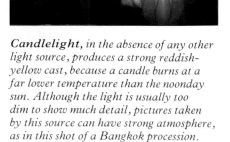

Candlelight, in the absence of any other light source, produces a strong reddish-yellow cast, because a candle burns at a far lower temperature than the noonday sun. Although the light is usually too dim to show much detail, pictures taken by this source can have strong atmosphere, as in this shot of a Bangkok procession.

At sunrise and sunset, *natural light is at its reddest because the light has to travel farther through the atmosphere. As a result, many short blue wavelengths are absorbed, allowing the longer red wavelengths to predominate. Below, the sunset sky has tinged the gray rocks of the Grand Canyon with red light.*

At noon, *with a few white clouds, daylight is neutral in color. Because this is the light for which most films are balanced, the colors of objects under noon sunlight look correct. The picture of kites on a beach was taken in these conditions – and shows pure whites and reds in the nearest kite.*

In the shade, *photographs often have a strong blue cast, because objects are illuminated only by light reflected from the blue sky, and receive no direct sunlight. Overcast skies also usually produce bluish colors. Here, a cool blue light suffuses both the white ibis and the water.*

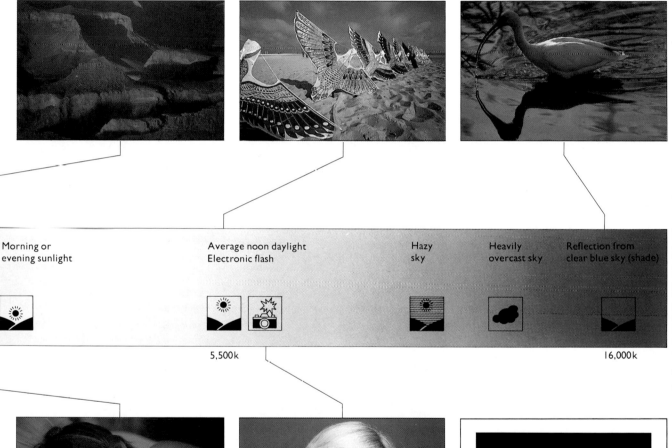

Morning or evening sunlight

Average noon daylight
Electronic flash

Hazy sky

Heavily overcast sky

Reflection from clear blue sky (shade)

5,500k   16,000k

Household bulbs *burn hotter than candles, but produce a much yellower light than does the sun. This means that with ordinary daylight film in the camera, pictures taken in room lighting usually have an overall orange cast. The picture of a sleeping child shows that the warm effect of this light can suit skin tones.*

Electronic flash *is balanced to match the color temperature of noon daylight. Thus, you can use it safely indoors or out, without creating color casts. Had this studio flash portrait been taken by the light of tungsten photographic lamps, a special slide film (described overleaf) would have been needed.*

Fluorescent light
This does not belong on the color temperature scale because it is not a burning light source. The color casts it produces vary greatly. Above, the greenish lights of an airport runway give the Concorde a surreal look.

The balance of color/2

Not many situations in photography call for any special measures to cope with the color quality of the light. Most pictures are taken outdoors by the light of the sky or sun, and slight variations in color caused by weather conditions or time of day often add pictorial interest rather than cause problems (see pages 132-35). But sometimes a light source produces a color mixture too far removed from the lighting for which your film is intended. When this happens, unacceptable color casts may appear in the picture – for example, green flesh tones in a portrait. You can avoid this situation either by choosing special film or by using filters to modify the light as it enters the lens. Color print films have a fair tolerance to different kinds of light because corrections can be made in processing, but with slide film the balance is crucial.

A special slide film is available for shooting indoors under tungsten bulbs. However, this film is balanced for powerful lamps used in photography studios, and will not entirely remove the unnatural color cast produced by ordinary, lower-watt bulbs. Alternatively, conversion and light-balancing filters are available in a complete range of colors, including those for fluorescent lighting. Some of the most useful filters are demonstrated on these two pages.

Daylight and film balance
Most color films, print and slide, are designed to work best in daylight, accurately reproducing the colors we see (right). Almost all the film you use will be balanced for daylight. The exception is slide film balanced for tungsten lighting. This film has a bluer quality overall, rendering a scene lit by orange light from tungsten lamps as near white. Used in ordinary daylight, the film produces unnatural blues (far right).

1 – Daylight with daylight film

2 – with tungsten film

Tungsten light and film balance
In tungsten light, whether from ordinary bulbs or special tungsten photographic lamps, film balanced for daylight records an orange or yellow cast (right). Although the warm color can be attractive, this is not how we see the scene. For more accurate results, the light can be partly corrected with a bluish No. 80A filter (far right, above). However, for greater accuracy, use slide film balanced for tungsten light (far right, below).

1 – Tungsten light with daylight film

2 – with No. 80A filter

3 – with tungsten film

Filtering fluorescent light

Although fluorescent lamps look white to the eye, they produce an unpredictable variety of color casts on film – ranging through yellow, blue or green. The scene in an airport control tower at right has a distinctly greenish cast from the fluorescent tubes. A fluorescent filter (far right) does not balance the light perfectly to the daylight film. but does give a warmer, more natural look.

1 – Fluorescent light with daylight film

2 – with fluorescent filter

Filtering overcast daylight

Heavy clouds scatter the shorter blue wavelengths of sunlight, raising the color temperature of the light and producing a blue cast on film (right). This still-life was rephotographed with a No. 81B pink filter to reduce the proportion of blue (far right). Many photographers use this filter as a matter of course on cloudy days.

1 – Overcast daylight with daylight film

2 – with No. 81B filter

Corrective printing: tungsten light

Filtration control in printing may restore accurate colors to print film. The portrait photographed in household tungsten light (right) has a strong orange cast. By asking the printer for a reprint with corrective filtration, (far right), the photographer secured a much more accurate result.

1– Tungsten light, uncorrected

2 – with corrective printing

Corrective printing: fluorescent light

The green cast from fluorescent light is more obtrusive than the orange from tungsten lamps. This portrait, shot by the light from fluorescent tubes in an office (right), has an unpleasant color if uncorrected. When asked to compensate. the printer produced an improvement (far right), but has not succeeded in imitating the natural colors of a daylit scene.

1 – Fluorescent light, uncorrected

2 – with corrective printing

PICTURES OF OURSELVES

The first pictures any photographer takes are likely to be of people. When they are of family or friends, the most popular subjects, they have a personal meaning that can move us because they record our own lives. But whether the subject is familiar or not, the pictures that we turn to most often do more than simply record what people look like. Instead, they reveal what is individual about the subjects, and perhaps what they are feeling. The portraits on the following pages all exhibit this special quality.

Pictures of people close to us can have a direct emotional impact because the photographer can reveal insights impossible to a casual observer, and catch moments that could never be staged. Yet strong, spontaneous pictures such as the one opposite are relatively rare. Although friends and relatives are convenient subjects, they can also be among the most difficult to photograph well. The first section that follows will suggest ways of avoiding pitfalls, so that your pictures give the impression of having been snatched from life. And it will show you how to capture candid glimpses of people in a variety of settings.

Even more challenging is a formally posed portrait, especially if it is of someone you hardly know. You must quickly establish a basic understanding of character and a mutual confidence. You must decide what surroundings and lighting will suit your subject. And then you must find a pose that is telling, yet lets the subject feel at ease. The same need for consideration and control applies to nude photography. The sections on portraits and nudes show how you can extend your skill and creativity in these areas, both of which require special planning.

A burly police officer with
*his baby shows the power of a
simple, direct portrait. Their
mutual delight is heightened
by contrasts – between the
father's leather-jacketed
toughness and his gentle
pride; and between his big
hands and the tiny body he
is cradling so securely.*

The unposed elegance *of a fledgling ballerina is captured in this delightful informal picture, taken while the child was lost in thought. A moment later the expression might have changed. Soft light from the window is perfect for the delicate skin tones of her limbs.*

143

The loving glance of a husband at his wife says everything about their amiable relationship. The couple's son took the picture from behind the bench while they were waiting for him to load the camera for a more posed photograph.

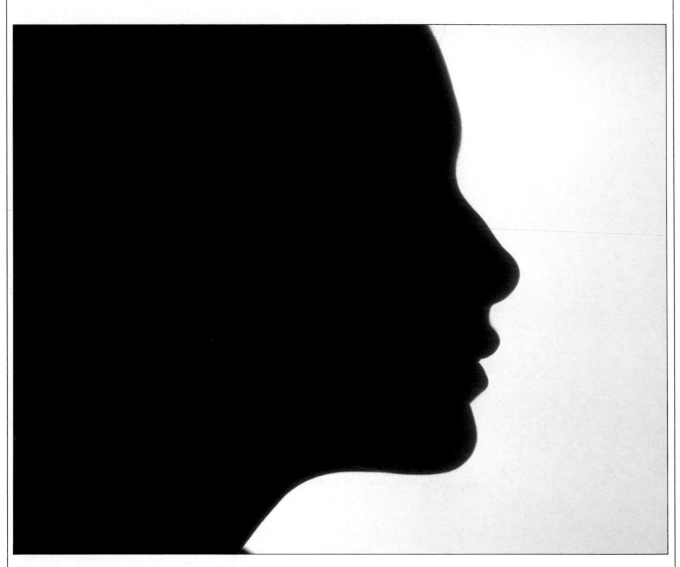

Simplified shape – *the flowing outline of a girl's profile silhouetted against a light background – is the only element in this highly graphic portrait. Backlighting deliberately excludes every surface detail.*

Strong modeling of form
*was needed in this picture to
bring out the expressive force
of a Kickapoo Indian's face.
The photographer used light
from windows on two sides
of a small room to carve
the man's chunky features.*

An old Mexican *relaxes in golden evening sunlight. The photographer positioned the subject outdoors in familiar surroundings to achieve this natural portrait. Yet the warm light of the low sun is as effective as any that a studio set-up could provide.*

A gaudy red room provides an apt
setting for a painter sitting below one of
her pictures – a pastiche of Velazquez's
celebrated Venus. The photographer
posed her to echo the picture, and used
a single, large studio flash unit.

Suspended bird-like *above the swimming pool, a friend of the photographer's appears in a spectacular and memorable head-on view. The picture was one of several taken as the girl practiced the dive.*

Two friends, *a glitter of spray and the outline of a surfboard encapsulate the mood of a summer day in this tightly composed telephoto lens picture.*

A rugged profile (*left*), obliquely lit and in close-up, displays a classic simplicity. Deliberate underexposure has increased the dramatic, high-contrast effect.

A steelworker (*above*) stands in the glow of the furnace he tends. By using this fiery, unnatural light, the photographer shows the hardship of the job and the stolid toughness of the man.

The romantic mood *of this simple nude comes from the use of soft light from a large window, a relaxed pose and an unpretentious setting. The picture's easy naturalness belies its careful planning.*

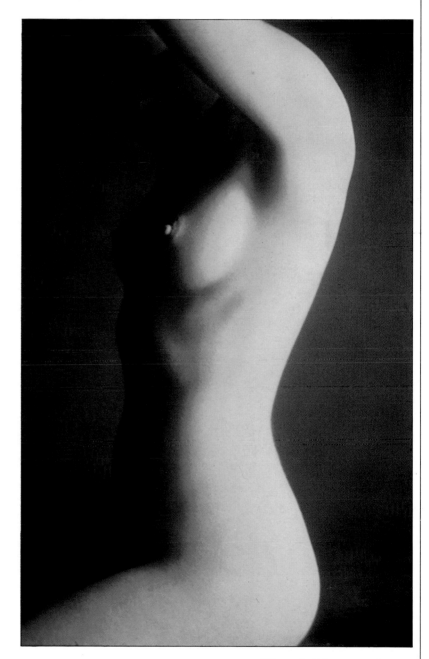

These full forms and *classic lines appear almost as a sculpture in light. The photographer used a strong studio photolamp, diffused by a plastic screen and angled to stress the curved outline.*

153

Seated on a rock above a
pool of clear water, a girl
becomes part of her setting.
The photographer framed the
scene to exclude the sky and
concentrate on the contrast
between her smooth body and
the roughness of the rock.

An athletic black body
(right) lies stretched out in a
surreal landscape – in fact
Utah's salt flats at sunset.
Deliberate underexposure has
increased the harsh contrast
in a nude of expressive and
elemental power.

PEOPLE AT THEIR BEST

Taking good pictures of people in their daily lives requires some forethought – it is surprisingly easy to end up with a muddled image, or one in which the subject looks bored, listless or wooden. What people really want is a picture that brings out their individuality and shows that they are alive. Whether you are taking the most informal snapshot or carefully recording a family occasion such as a wedding, your aim should be to capture the essence of a subject's personality as reflected in a particular situation. Such clarity comes from knowing in advance what you want an image to portray, and then achieving this in the simplest and most direct way.

The following pages explore techniques for obtaining the best from people – from getting them to appear more natural to placing them in the right light. You can then reach past the barriers that even friends and family put up before the camera, and past the clutter of surroundings, to arrive at whatever is distinctive about the character of your subject.

The halo of light around a girl's tousled red-gold hair seems to embody the warmth of her laughter. By getting the subject to swing round suddenly, the photographer obtained a spontaneous and perfectly relaxed picture. Since the girl's face is out of the sun, there is no squint to mar the effect.

Expressing personality

Faces – especially the faces of people we know – are supremely eloquent guides to personality. Any photographer realizes the advantage of a vivid expression or gesture. Because of this, it is easy to forget that other elements in a picture also provide valuable clues to character.

Everything included in the final image can help in building an impression of the subject, from a person's hairstyle, dress and way of sitting or standing, to pieces of furniture and other objects – indeed the entire setting. Just by placing your subjects in a sympathetic environment, you can reveal something of their personalities. In the two close-ups below on the right, the colors of outdoor settings serve to reinforce the healthy appearance of the subjects. To take such spontaneous pictures, you need to decide in advance what aspect of your subject's character you want to emphasize, and then be on hand with a loaded camera until the moment you are waiting for presents itself.

Photographing people with their favorite possessions will speak volumes about their personalities. You do not need to clutter the picture with objects to get the message across: the best portraits are often those in which the photographer has singled out just a few telling details that seem to encapsulate a person's attitudes and lifestyle. Again, you should plan in advance what you want the picture to say about your subject. The carefully posed portrait on the opposite page is a classic example of how selected details can be strikingly used to express individual personality.

The tanned complexion and windswept hair of this girl, framed by a background of blue sky and water, convey simply but powerfully the independence and vitality of a fresh-air enthusiast.

A style-aware teenager props a shoulder against a boutique window. The girl's defiant attitude, the split image of her reflection, even the eye-catching motif on her shirt, combine to give an image full of character and vitality.

Radiating zest for life, this informal portrait taken at a ski resort acquires additional sparkle from the clean, bright background of the snow. The off-center position of the shot and the angle of the head help to suggest an easy-going, extraverted personality.

Quizzical good humor is pointedly evoked by this study of an old man. The subject's formal pose, and the outmoded decor and dress all reveal a life rich in memories.

Relaxing the subject

Even your closest friends and immediate family – people who are normally quite at ease in your company – can freeze up suddenly when you aim a camera at them. The resulting picture may look stilted and unnatural.

Every photographer has to cope with camera shyness at some time. How you go about relaxing the subject depends partly on what type of person you are dealing with, partly on your relationship with him, and partly on the situation. To a certain extent, you will have to extemporize – but there are some advance preparations you can make. Get the technicalities out of the way well before the portrait session: decide which exposure, lighting angle and camera viewpoint you want – using a stand-in for the subject if necessary – and prefocus whenever this is possible. Unless you are confident of your technique, you are likely to seem nervous, and this will make your subject feel uncomfortable.

Think about props, too. One of the best ways of putting people at ease is to divert their attention from the camera. Giving your subject something to do will help, as in the pictures below of the boy playing with his father's pipe. Adolescents, particularly, tend to appear self-conscious and uncomfortable in portraits. Try to find a situation or setting that will give the subjects confidence.

If you are photographing a couple who enjoy a close relationship, such as the father and son shown here, you may find them becoming so absorbed in each other that they forget the camera completely. Such happy situations are more likely to develop if you remain as unobtrusive as possible. A telephoto lens allows you to distance yourself from your subjects, but still close in on any aspect of their image that catches your eye.

Engrossed in a game with a pipe, the father and son in the two pictures above are completely oblivious to the camera. The use of a 135mm telephoto lens has allowed the photographer to stay back and focus only on the smiling profiles, closely linked, and delicately rimmed by the sunlight.

With the boy relaxed (right), the photographer moved back farther to get a picture that showed more of the setting. The out-of-focus foliage adds to the soft, mellow mood of each of the photographs, and helps to create the sense that the father and son are occupying a private world.

At work and play

We define people as much by what they do as by the way they look, and friends or relatives engaged in activities, whether at work or play, make excellent subjects for informal photographs. Such pictures can reveal fresh facets of personality in someone we know well – and they often succeed in bringing a person to life when a more orthodox and straightforward portrait would fail to do so.

This is true particularly if your subject tends to be ill at ease before a camera, or has a reserved personality that is difficult to draw out in a posed picture. The great advantage of photographing people intent on what they are doing is that they are unselfconscious. In addition, shared absorption in a hobby, task or game makes it easier to capture a relationship between people. The pictures here of friends tussling over a basketball, of a young fisherman with his grandfather, and of a camera-shy farmer shearing a sheep, are all examples of people who are completely in their element, and therefore at their most natural and authentic.

Remember that the activity itself will provide more than enough visual interest – so keep the background simple and concentrate on a few selected details. Pictures of children playing are particularly difficult to organize coherently, and you may find that a high viewpoint helps to separate the figures, as in the picture below.

An overhead view of three friends playing basketball has brought clarity to what might have been a confusing picture. The triangular shape of the figures with the colored ball at the apex, is well placed in the frame, and emphasized by the plain, square tiles. Yet the outstretched fingers and straining expressions of the boys still capture the feeling of movement.

The art of shrimp netting absorbs a boy and his grandfather at the seaside. The intent concentration of the pair excludes the camera's presence – an effect the photographer helped by the use of a telephoto lens. A shallow depth of field has kept the subjects and the reflections in the wet sand sharp while blurring the breakwater and the pier in the background of the picture.

A shaft of light focuses attention on the balanced shapes of two faces, one bent down over his task, the other tilting upward. The photographer respected the shearer's reluctance to have a formal portrait taken, and by waiting quietly, captured this telling picture of strength, experience and care. The simple stone wall contrasts well with the sheep's woolly coat.

163

The right lens

Catching a telling expression or pose is the key to many successful pictures of people. But choice of lens may play an important part in determining the composition and impact of the picture. A standard 50mm or 55mm lens – excellent for half- or full-length portraits – has the outstanding merit of showing people in a natural scale with one another and with their surroundings. Yet you can expand your creative range when photographing people by trying lenses with longer or shorter focal lengths, especially for certain subjects.

A telephoto lens has two distinct qualities that make it useful. First, its magnifying effect allows you to stay well back so that you can fill the frame with a head-and-shoulders portrait without crowding the subject. And second, the shallow depth of field of this lens becomes a particular asset in portraiture, when often you want to blur a confusing background so as to provide a plain frame for the main subject. A lens with a focal length of 200mm or larger can be used, but those of 85mm to 135mm give a more pleasing perspective – and are certainly easier to handle.

Wide-angle lenses come into their own when, conversely, you want to include background or foreground details in the picture – either because the setting is interesting or because it supplies a kind of commentary on the character or interests of the subject. Moderately wide-angle lenses are the most useful, particularly those with focal lengths of 28mm or 35mm. Their broad angles of view and great depth of field mean that you can show sharp details of a subject's environment, whether these details are close to the lens or distant.

A wide-angle lens has special advantages when you are photographing large groups. You can fit everybody into the frame without going so far back that the faces and expressions become lost. Sometimes, too, the tendency of wide-angle lenses to distort perspective at close range can be used creatively, as in the picture of the boy on the right, who is challenging all comers to invade his private territory in a tree house.

An old man's head looks as grand and imposing as a biblical prophet's, an effect helped by the close framing and shallow depth of field of a 200mm telephoto lens. The distance from which you can get close-ups with this lens allows the subject to remain relaxed.

A huge mural dominates the boy's solitary ball game in this unusual picture, taken with a standard lens. The sense of scale would have been less impressive with another focal length: a wide-angle lens would have made the wall appear smaller, and a telephoto lens would have included only part of the scene.

The boy's feet and legs, as shown by a wide-angle lens, seem to expand to fill the space of his tree house, suggesting his aggressive authority in his own domain.

165

The ideal light

Bright sun and blue sky may seem ideal conditions for photography, but they are seldom good for photographing people. Strong sunlight is too intense to show subtleties of skin tones and texture, and from some angles the harsh light can turn fine lines of character into deep wrinkles. The high sun of noon has particularly unattractive effects, putting deep shadows under a subject's nose and chin and making the eyes sink into dark hollows. In these conditions, look for an area of open shade with enough soft, reflected illumination to light your subject adequately.

The weaker sunlight of morning and evening is much better. Even so, people will find difficulty in facing the sun with their eyes relaxed and open, and you should try to place them so that the light falls on their faces at an angle of about 45. The soft reddish light of evening warming a tanned face and glinting in the subject's eyes can convey the glow of a summer's day more effectively than the harsh light of noonday, as the amusing and inventive group photograph below shows.

If you want to use oblique directional daylight to bring out the strength of a face, thin clouds or haze will help to diffuse the sunlight and reveal some form. Thicker clouds go farther in diffusing the light, and provide gentle modeling of a face, as is evident in the picture of the old lady opposite with a sheaf of wheat. In addition, overcast weather eases the technical problem of choosing an exposure to suit both highlight and shadow areas without losing detail in either. The ideal illumination is the broad, even light of an overcast day, which is muted but not dull – this kind of light reveals detail clearly but does not create the hard shadows that can ruin a picture. Less-intense light also enables you to open up the aperture so as to reduce depth of field if you need to blur out a background.

Fishing nets on the beach frame an unusual group portrait in which the low evening sun tinges the faces with warm orange light. Harsher noon sunlight would have shown less texture in the nets, and cast obscuring shadows.

Harvest home, and proud of her ability to help, this elderly farmer's wife stands in light diffused by heavy clouds, so that only soft shadows play over her lined face. The fine detail shows what effective pictures can be taken in this light. To offset the blue color tinge that overcast weather often produces on slide film, the photographer used a No. 81A pale yellow conversion filter.

A lazy day by the sea comes to an end for a beach sitter as hazy clouds reduce the intensity of the afternoon sun. The pale, even light and muted colors helped the photographer to capture a picture that evokes the atmosphere perfectly.

Backlight and silhouettes

Backlighting, with the light coming from behind the subject, changes our view of a person dramatically by emphasizing the outlines, rather than the detailed forms, of faces and figures. Because people can be identified by outlines alone, when you know them well the results of backlighting can be distinctive and intriguing – a combination of familiarity and mystery.

Depending on the strength and source of light, and the exposure, you can create very different effects with backlighting. Intense light produces dark, almost two-dimensional silhouettes, like those of the children in the photograph below, if you take the meter reading for the bright background. When there is also some frontal lighting – either direct or reflected – you can retain some of the details in silhouetted shapes. For example, in the picture on the opposite page, the photographer chose an exposure that allowed strong sunlight reflected through the window to reveal the delicate tone of the girls' skin. If the sun is not directly behind the subject, the result may be a silhouette ringed with light. Rim lighting, as it is known, imparts a radiant warmth, particularly suited to romantic portraits such as the one on the right.

The aura of light *around an embracing couple adds to the romantic intensity of this close-up photograph, while the silhouetting of the figures conveys the impression of a private moment.*

Children playing on a jetty
(left) are transformed into
almost hieroglyphic figures
by strong backlighting. The
photographer set an exposure
for the lighter background,
underexposing the figures to
obtain the black silhouettes
and monochromatic setting.

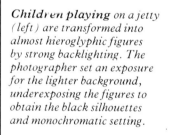

The willowy profiles of
two sisters are backlit by
sunlight delicately filtering
through curtains. Reflected
light from the window gently
dapples the girls' soft skin
and picks out details in the
silhouettes, while the shape
of the alcove accentuates the
subjects' long, slender limbs.

Modifying the light

For photographing people indoors, no source of lighting is as natural and convenient as the daylight coming through a window or an open door. Usually the light is reasonably bright, with none of the color-balance problems of household lighting.

However, unless the room has large windows on more than one wall, window light tends to be strongly directional. If you do not take steps to modify the light, half of your subject's face may come out bright and the other half in deep shadow. Occasionally, this can be an advantage. For the picture below, the photographer deliberately restricted the light from a sunlit window to a narrow beam. As a result, the contrast of light and shade draws attention to the strong lines of her friend's face and chin.

More often, you will want to avoid stark differences between highlight and shadow areas. Strong contrast makes it difficult to select the best exposure for showing natural skin tones or for revealing the subtleties of facial form. One way of reducing contrast is to reflect some of the light streaming through the window back toward the shaded side of your subject's face. For example, the book the child is reading in the picture at the top of this page not only makes a natural prop but also serves the very practical function of lightening shadows on her face. Alternatively, you may be able to place your subject closer to a light-colored internal wall that will reflect back some light.

Softening the light from the window can also help to mute the brighter part of a scene, so that you can increase the exposure and show more detail in the shadows. Lace curtains or translucent blinds will help to diffuse the daylight entering the room. An equally effective diffusion technique is to pin a bed-sheet or tracing paper across the window frame.

A young reader sits by a window, and bright sunlight flooding into the room gives her hair a halo of light. Unmodified, the strong back-lighting would have thrown her face into deep shadow. However, the photographer used her book to bounce back some sunlight and soften the harsh contrast.

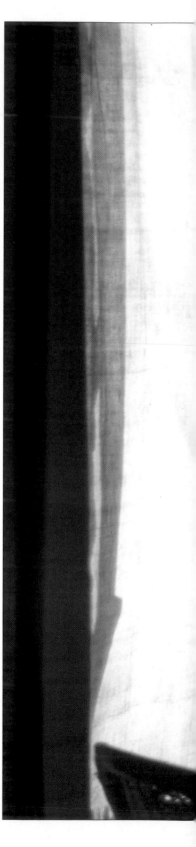

Peering from shadows, the young woman at left leans into a pool of light. The photographer needed some way of excluding from this picture the over-cluttered surroundings of the room. She pulled heavy curtains and moved in close for a strong picture that uses just a chink of light.

Young cardplayers sit by
a window with a thin curtain,
which diffused the sunlight
enough to allow an exposure
setting balanced between
the highlights and shadows.

Using flash

An electronic flash unit is a highly useful source of light, but perched on top of the camera, pointing directly forward, much of its potential may be wasted. Pictures taken with the flash in the accessory shoe can look harsh and unnatural — portraits may appear unflattering, because flash, when it is aimed directly in line with the camera, seems to flatten the subject's features.

There are two solutions to this problem. The simplest is to move the flash off the accessory shoe and hold it above or to one side of the camera. To do this, you need a flash cord. Basic types plug into a socket on the camera body and synchronize the flash with the shutter. More advanced types — for use with modern, computer-controlled cameras — have an attachment that slots onto the camera's accessory shoe. Electrical contacts on the attachment link up with those on the accessory shoe and allow exposure information to pass between the camera and the flash.

To provide modeling illumination, point the flash straight toward the subject, but at an angle from the camera. It is easier to do this if you use a long cord and get someone to hold the flash for you.

The other way to improve flash pictures is to use a flash unit with a tilting head, and bounce the light off a reflective surface, such as a white-painted wall or ceiling. This method produces very soft lighting.

For correct exposure with bounce flash using a manual flash unit, calculate the total distance from the tilted flash head to the ceiling and from the ceiling to the subject. Use the exposure table on the flash to find the "correct" aperture for this distance, then set an aperture two stops wider than this — the wider aperture setting compensates for the light that's absorbed by the ceiling.

Self-regulating and dedicated flash units set the correct exposure automatically. With a self-regulating flash, set the largest automatic aperture option and ensure that the sensor cell is pointed directly at your subject when you make an exposure.

If your flash unit has a second head, turn it on for bounce flash exposures. The low strength flash from this head fills-in shadows cast by the main flash and puts an attractive catchlight in your subject's eyes. You can achieve the same effect if you fix a piece of white card to the top of the main flash head. When the flash fires, most of the light bounces off the ceiling, but some of it bounces off the card and directly onto your subject.

Bounce flash has certain limitations — in rooms with high or dark ceilings there is a danger of underexposure. Similarly, it cannot be used in rooms with colored walls or ceilings, as the reflected light takes on the color of the reflective surface. In such cases, try bouncing the flash off a large, white board.

Sparkling highlights give this impromptu portrait a party atmosphere. By taking the flash unit off the camera, the photographer was able to move the shadows to one side, and avoid the flat lighting that flash can produce when mounted on the camera.

Flash off the camera
Hold the flash at arm's length, and point it toward the subject. You need a long flash cord, and it helps if you have someone to hold the flash for you at an appropriate angle.

The natural look of the portrait above comes not from daylight, but from bounce flash. With the flash unit pointed at the ceiling, the light reaching the subject is diffused, soft, and even – perfect for portraits.

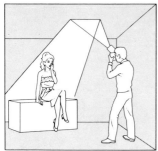

Bouncing flash
Choose a wide aperture setting and tilt the flash unit's head upward. This technique works best when the subject is close, and the ceiling or reflective surface is low and white.

Fill-in flash
Bright sunlight casts deep shadows, which can be particularly unflattering for portraits. A flash unit can "lift" the shadows, as the pictures below show. But for a natural look, the flash power needs to be reduced to about half its normal strength.

With dedicated units, the flash uses exposure information from the camera's meter to set the fill-in flash level automatically. On some units, a flash exposure compensation control allows you to alter the brightness of the fill-in illumination.

On self-regulating units you have to "trick" the flash into acting as though your film is faster than it really is. For a half strength burst of flash, set the film speed on the unit to double the speed of the film in the camera. Then, set the smallest automatic aperture option on the lens and take a meter reading. Check that the recommended shutter speed is the same as, or slower than, the camera's flash synchronization speed. Finally, reduce the aperture by a half-stop to adjust for the extra light from the flash.

Without flash

With fill-in flash

173

Toddlers

Toddlers have none of the inhibitions that often make it difficult to photograph adults. In fact, the main problem is keeping them at arm's length for a photograph. Like any glittering, shiny object, a camera appeals to a child's curiosity, and if you are not careful you may find your lens covered with small sticky fingerprints.

You can get around this problem in several ways. The simplest is to use the element of surprise. Because young children become totally absorbed in activity, you should find it easy to sneak up unobserved. Before you get anywhere near, set the camera to programmed or semi-automatic exposure mode. If you haven't got an autofocus camera, pre-focus the lens for a distance of about three feet and move in quietly until the viewfinder image is sharp. Then, attract the child's attention before releasing the shutter. The wide-eyed expression of surprise on the face of the child in the small picture below is typical of the spontaneous reactions you can capture.

Another technique is to use a telephoto lens and compose the picture farther away from the toddler. This has the added advantage that the increased distance between you and your subject results in a more accurate perspective. Children's heads are bigger in relation to their bodies than are adults' heads, and a standard or wide-angle lens can some-times exaggerate this. A telephoto lens restores the balance and gives a more natural effect.

The camera position also affects perspective and proportion. Seen from above, children's heads are closer than their feet to the camera – and therefore look bigger on film. Rather than standing up to take the picture, try kneeling or lying on the ground to produce a more intimate and revealing child's-eye view of your small subjects.

Sucking her thumb, a little girl stares with surprise at her father's camera. For taking pictures such as this by available light indoors, a medium-speed film such as ISO 100 is not sensitive enough. Instead, use an ISO 400 film so that you can freeze the child's movement with a fast shutter speed, instead of having to resort to a flash, which can be alarming if the burst of light is unexpected (1/125 at f/2).

A sunlit deck chair seems as big as a hammock to a two-year-old boy (right). The photographer successfully conveys this sense of scale by composing the picture in such a way that the top of the chair hides half of the child's face, and the striped fabric envelopes his body.

174

On the seashore, *this little girl is relaxed for the camera. By getting down to her level, instead of standing up, the photographer has made a more intimate, natural picture, and included the surf and horizon in the background.*

Brothers, sisters and friends

Most children are naturally gregarious. Surrounded by their brothers and sisters, or among their friends, their confidence blossoms. Whereas a child alone may be painfully awkward in front of the camera, several together may delight in performing for you.

Often, getting a good picture of children together means finding a midpoint between an overly formal pose and the disjointed effect of allowing the subjects total freedom. With a large group, a useful technique is to arrange them in a fairly structured way, and then wait for them to break the pose. Enough of the original formation will survive to give shape to the image, but the effect will be lively and spontaneous. Another approach is to encourage a boisterous game, joining in at first but then slipping away to take some pictures when the fun becomes unstoppable. Usually you will not need to contrive the action; children playing together will soon present you with a lively composition.

The developing relationships between children are a rewarding aspect of childhood that you will want to include in the family album. If you have more than one child, the emotional closeness, the shared joys and the little dramas of brothers and sisters will have a special meaning to you. To capture these moments on film, a telephoto lens can prove particularly useful – perhaps a 135mm or 200mm telephoto, or a 80-200mm zoom lens. With these, you will be able to close in on the children's private world from a distance and catch intimate expressions, as in the picture of a sister and brother at the bottom of the opposite page. Try to set them against a plain background, or else wait until the children are close together to frame them tightly.

Friends at ballet class rest
before practice. The careful
composition focuses on one
particular girl, but the angle
of her gaze directs the viewer
to the others in the group.

Boys show off their daring at an adventure playground. By panning the camera at 1/30, the photographer kept the main subject's features sharp and conveyed the action.

In mock aggression, a girl responds to her brother's teasing grab at her mirror. The closeness of the two smiling profiles points up the family resemblance.

Parents and grandparents

Stereotyping is a special pitfall to avoid when taking photographs of the senior members of the family. Without thinking, we tend to portray the father as the head of the household, cast the mother in the caring role, and accord grandparents a sedate setting that befits the dignity or frailty of their years. You will produce more interesting pictures – and please the subjects too – if you regard older relatives not in terms of their family positions or as representatives of a type-cast generation, but as individuals, each offering different photographic possibilities.

Remember that your family has a life outside the home. The most expressive pictures of parents and grandparents are often taken when they escape their domestic surroundings. Pictures of a grandfather striding across the golf course or, as here, a grandmother riding her bicycle remind us not to equate age with staidness. Emotions, too, can be portrayed eloquently. The picture on the opposite page expresses love as powerfully as any image of a young honeymoon couple could. The close cropping of the image wastes nothing; and yet the color of the man's lined face – sharply revealed by the strong sun – finds an echo in a blur of autumn leaves in the background. Such pictures are effective because they challenge our preconceptions about older people.

Parents tend to relax in the familiar surroundings of their home, and to react delightedly to the picture-taking efforts of their own children. This couple's son caught them perfectly.

An affectionate hug (*left*) and the man's response seem to encapsulate a lifetime of love in this study of a weatherbeaten couple. The picture's strength lies in its spontaneity and its absolute economy.

A sense of unabated fun shines from this picture of a trim grandmother. The soft, diffused light that filters through the leaves flatters the subject's silver-gray hair and rosy skin tones.

Wedding day/1

At a wedding, a photographer has few second chances – often there is just one opportunity to get everything right. However, there are some simple ways to reduce the risk of disappointment. One of these is the choice of film. Fast color print film (ISO 400) has exceptional tolerance to errors of overexposure, and its great sensitivity gives you the maximum chance of taking pictures indoors by available light, as in the beautiful example below.

In case the light in the church is too dim for a picture even with fast film, a small flash unit is advisable. Also, for portraits, extra light from a flash can help to reduce the tonal contrast between the groom's dark clothes and the bride's white dress: move the groom slightly closer to the camera than the bride, so the flash lights him more brilliantly.

If the weather is good, you will want to take some pictures outdoors. But try to photograph groups in the shade rather than making them face the harshness of direct sunlight. Alternatively, position them with the light behind, and take a close reading. If you have to take pictures in direct sun, be careful of shadows caused by hats. Either move the group so that some light falls on the faces or use a flash at reduced power to fill in the shadows.

Choose a moderately wide-angle lens rather than a standard lens. A 35mm lens, such as the one used for the picture of the bride at right, lets you get closer to the subject in a tight space, and also reduces the chance of a guest walking in front of the camera just at the moment of exposure and thereby ruining your photograph.

A sunlit church calls for careful metering. Here, the large windows and reflective white walls provided plenty of natural light, but the photographer gave one stop more exposure than indicated to compensate for the bright windows in the background.

*A **nervous bride*** *waits in the church entrance. Even in some large churches, certain areas tend to be relatively cramped. For this picture, the photographer had to use a wide-angle lens in order to encompass all of the flowing lines of the wedding dress.*

*A **wedding cake*** *sometimes appears as a featureless white shape if the picture is taken with direct flash on the camera. To avoid this, the photographer pointed the flash at a white wall on the left, to soften the light, and opened up two stops.*

The snapshot style

Candid pictures do not need the polished technique and perfect composition of more considered types of photography. On the contrary, the imperfections of the hastily taken snapshot – figures awkwardly cut off by the frame, elements out of focus, inaccuracies in exposure – can actually add to the sense of reality and authenticity. They stress the picture's immediacy as a spontaneous image – the record of a passing moment in real life.

The impact of the pictures on these two pages comes from their content rather than their purely photographic qualities. They show how the photographer's alert eye and quick reactions to an action or expression can capture a little slice of life. Even if you do not adopt this approach as a permanent style, you can use it occasionally. When you see something interesting that you know will last for only a second, do not hesitate. Take the picture fast, without even thinking of the technical considerations. You will be surprised at the number of worthwhile photographs you get – images that otherwise would have been missed altogether.

An inflated tire tube provides a youngster with a makeshift sled. A shutter speed of 1/1000 stopped the boy's motion, the excitement of the image more than compensating for the very close framing.

A spontaneous gesture as the groom lifts up the bride conveys the warmth of the moment. The liveliness of the photograph outweighs its technical flaws – the crooked verticals, the figure intruding from the right and the background that is neither very sharp nor wholly blurred.

A bathing beauty (above) makes a call from a phone-booth near the shore. A quick snapshot caught the incongruity of the moment.

A traffic cop (above) calls a halt. Using a standard lens, the photographer simply crouched down quickly and recorded the expression.

Two friends (left) leap over a row of wooden posts in spontaneous play. The photographer, relying on fast reactions rather than technical skill, snapped the scene before it passed.

187

Faces in the crowd

Turning your camera on the spectators can provide pictures as lively and fascinating as those of the event itself. Make a habit of scanning the crowds every so often, looking out for interesting faces. People cheering on their favorite team, or anxious about the outcome of a feat of daring, or simply waiting for the action to begin, make marvelous subjects for candid photography.

If you are some distance away – perhaps facing a crowd on the other side of a street or stadium – a telephoto lens is very useful. The shallow depth of field and narrow view enable you to pick an individual out of a group or mass of people and to throw surrounding or background details out of focus, as in the two pictures on this page. A long lens is also handy because the compressed perspective can encompass a whole range of facial expressions, as at bottom right, where reactions vary from mild involvement to intense emotion.

If you are in the midst of a crowd, take advantage of your position by looking for interesting subjects close to you, but remember that you will probably have to aim and focus much more swiftly. A wide-angle lens is best for this purpose and lets you frame to include some elements of the surroundings, as in the carnival picture at right.

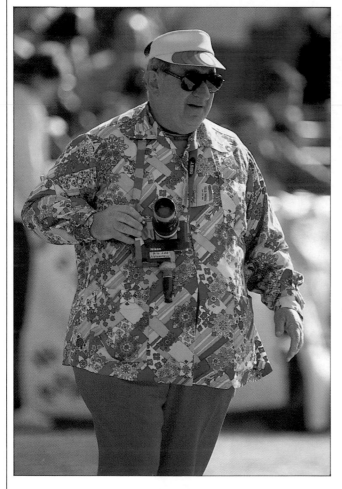

A flower girl seems disgruntled by a long wait in line during a Welsh music festival. The photographer noticed her frown and used the shallow depth of field of a long lens to pick out the face in sharp focus.

The flamboyant attire of a rotund photographer at the 1980 Superbowl in Pasadena provides a lively, colorful image. A 105 mm lens isolated the figure and left the busy background unfocused.

A Brazilian woman's vivacious grin seems to draw the viewer right into a carnival scene. The photographer spotted her when he was moving backward through the crowd, and used a 35mm lens to include the glittering hats behind.

The mixed reactions of spectators at a horserace in Calcutta, India (below), produced a fascinating study of human nature. The photographer closed in with a 200mm lens to compress the rows of excited faces.

Full-face or profile?

A full-face view can communicate with a viewer in a very direct way – perhaps through laughter or through the kind of challenging stare seen in the picture at left below. This approach can suit people with good eyes and regular features. But unless a sitter is confident and assertive, you risk the dullness of a passport photograph.

Profile views sometimes look excessively staged, and subjects may be wary of them because most people are not familiar with their own profiles. However, if you liven up the picture, as at right below, profile portraits can be unconventional and striking. This approach shows beautiful hair to advantage, especially with the head thrown back slightly to show the subject's long and graceful neck. In order to emphasize a profile, place the light ahead of the face and slightly farther back than the subject from the camera.

Three-quarter views, as shown in the picture on the opposite page, are in fact much more common in portraiture. They allow eye-contact with the camera, lost in a profile, and give a more relaxed impression than does a full-face portrait. Usually one side of a face looks better than the other, as models are well aware. If you are in doubt, take pictures from both sides and make a choice later. To achieve a natural pose, have your subject face slightly to one side and then look back toward the camera without any head movement. This contributes a hint of spontaneity, as if you have caught a personal glance. Keeping a conversation going will help subjects to relax, and a joke or smile may encourage similar responses. If not, suggest that the subjects stretch, shake their shoulders or even screw up their eyes. A smile may then appear quite naturally when you tell them to relax again.

A gray-eyed beauty fixes the camera with a cool stare. Careful makeup and wet hair simplify her face so that the eyes and mouth stand out.

A splash of water, frozen by an electronic flash, brings this simple profile to life. The girl's tilted head makes her neck seem longer.

A warm glance, backed up by a hint of a smile, gives this classic three-quarter portrait a relaxed and engaging intimacy. The photographer covered the lights with orange acetate for a bronze glow.

Candid portraits

In a formal portrait, the sitter's eyes are usually the most important feature, expressing character and providing a dominant point of interest. But unplanned portraits can also reveal this expressive quality, without losing the freshness and immediacy of truly candid pictures. In each of the portraits on these pages, the subject is looking directly at the camera, yet the effect is natural and unposed.

The secret of taking such photographs is, above all, to work quickly. A stranger owes you no obligation to cooperate while you set the camera's controls and find your viewpoint. Once your subject is aware of your intentions, any delay will result in unwanted posing, or else in awkwardness and perhaps resentment. Sometimes the best approach is to attract the subject's attention at the last moment – as in the picture at left below.

With a group of people, you can be more open. The man dominating the picture opposite, above, knew he was being photographed but not that he had been singled out from the crowd for a portrait. This image also shows how figures cropped by the edge of the frame strengthen the feeling of a grabbed photograph. In the large picture below, the foreground figure at one side seems included in the frame almost accidentally.

A French farmer looks up from his work with good-natured curiosity as he notices the camera. The photographer used a 28mm lens to include the neat rows of crops, and was all ready to press the shutter release as soon as the subject realized he was being photographed.

A strong face confronts the camera with an unflinching stare. Spotting the subject's cool, enigmatic expression in the midst of a crowd, the photographer closed in with a 105 mm lens at a wide aperture to throw the foreground out of focus. The frame edges cutting into the two out-of-focus faces give the picture movement, depth and immediacy.

A sidelong glance gives candid impact to this unusual portrait. The photographer chose a wide-angled lens and focused on the immediate foreground, using fill-in flash for good definition of the subject on an overcast day. The off-balanced framing suggests that the man has just appeared on the scene.

The outdoor portrait

Outdoor portraits have an appeal that is hard to match in a studio, particularly when you can use spontaneous incidents, as in the picture below, where a pigeon provided a natural prop. But you need to choose the right time of day. Early or late in the day, when the light falls obliquely on the subject, is a better time than at midday because the light is less harsh. If possible, plan your session for between one and three hours after sunrise or before sunset, although any time when the sun is below an angle of 45 degrees to the horizon will do. Next, decide how to place the subject in relation to the sun. Be prepared to move around to achieve the best balance of lighting and to include in the view-finder the least distracting background you can find. The diagrams on this page show some of the most effective positions.

The face, of course, is the most important part of a portrait. Make sure that you base your exposure on this, not on the background. To expose the face correctly, close right in and see what combination of aperture and shutter speed is indicated before moving back to your chosen camera position. Handheld meters are particularly useful for portraits. With some, you can take incident light readings by holding the meter just in front of the subject's face and pointing it back toward the camera. Measuring the light falling onto the subject by this method helps to ensure accurate recording of skin tones and color, whatever the brightness of the background or the tones of the subject's clothes. You may find that the light is insufficient for a handheld picture at an adequately fast shutter speed, in which case load up with a faster film or mount your camera on a tripod and ask your subject to adopt a pose that is comfortable and easy to maintain.

A young mother feeding a
pigeon shows how spontaneous
outdoor portraits can look,
even though this one was posed.

206

Controlling natural light

For portraits, you should take an active approach to sunlight, not just use it as you find it. Some of the examples below suggest advantageous times of day or how to move your subject into the best light. Others show how to modify the light falling onto the subject with reflectors of white cardboard or crumpled foil.

1 – With the sun diffused by haze or light clouds, you have near-ideal conditions for a soft and flattering portrait.

2 – With low, diffused sun, position your subject so that sidelighting creates strong modeling on the face.

3 – With harsh sunlight, place your subject in the shade, where the light will be more even and the shadows softer.

4 – With direct sunlight, place the subject near a large reflective surface to direct light back into the shadows.

5 – With strong, low sidelight, use a special curved reflector opposite the light to fill in areas of unwanted shadow.

6 – With the sun behind the subject, use a reflector to provide the main source of light falling onto the face.

Falling snow (right) is captured with a slow shutter speed of 1/30. In the example here the snow acted as a giant reflector, brightening the light even though the picture was taken late in the afternoon.

On the beach (right), harsh sunlight and reflected glare give an unpromising light. By turning the subject away from the sun and using a small hand mirror to reflect light back onto the girl's face, the photographer found an effective solution.

Bleak conditions (below) provided good shadowless light for a simple and direct portrait of an outdoor man. A wide aperture blurred out the background.

Natural light indoors

As a light source for portraiture, windows give a photographer a double advantage. Light from a window avoids any need for the studio apparatus that can make sitters anxious, and at the same time has a soft, natural quality that is very flattering. Using this simple light source, you can light a subject in countless different ways. The pictures below, with accompanying diagrams, show four main techniques, but there are many more. In each of the two large pictures at right, a window provided strong directional lighting. With the camera to one side of a window and the subject to the other side turned slightly toward the light, you can achieve excellent three-quarter portraits of this kind.

The crucial thing to remember about window lighting is that although the shadows are soft-edged, they can become deep and inky on the side of the head away from the light. In small or pale-colored rooms, the resulting contrast between light and dark may not be extreme because of light reflected off walls and ceiling onto the subject. But in a large room, or one with dark-colored carpets and furnishings, you may have to use a reflector to put some light back into the shadows. You can improvise a reflector from almost anything pale in color. Sheets of polystyrene are excellent, but even a book or sheet of newspaper will do. Shadows become softer as you move the reflector closer to the subject.

When the sun shines directly in through a window, the contrast increases dramatically, and you may need to soften the shadows by diffusing the light itself. You can do this by pinning a white bed sheet or a couple of thicknesses of artist's tracing paper across the window frame.

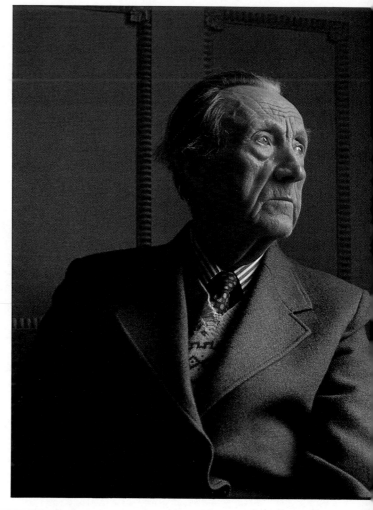

1 – Silhouette
The pictures with matching diagrams here show some of the ways you can use the light from a single window. With the camera facing the window and exposure based on the highlight, the subject is silhouetted (ISO 64: 1/125 at f/8).

2 – Backlighting
The arrangement was similar for this picture except that the photographer used a reflector to put light into the shadows. Exposure for the face bleached out the window highlight (ISO 64: 1 60 at f/4).

Looking back at a window, the poet Sacheverell Sitwell presents a strong character study. The soft, oblique light shows more form than would a frontal light.

Facing the camera, this young woman sits close to a window so that the light flows around her features, giving even tones. Tracing paper diffused the light.

3 – Rimlighting

Moving the subject's chair a little to the left makes a dramatic change. Whereas reflected backlighting was soft and flattering, this arrangement begins to reveal the real texture of the face (ISO 64: 1/60 at f/5.6).

4 – Frontal lighting

Moving the camera around to point into the room places the subject in more even, frontal light. The thin curtains were drawn to act as diffusers, softening the light on the subject's face (ISO 64: 1/60 at f/8).

Lighting faces/1

As a way of lighting faces, special photographic light is far easier to control than natural daylight. Even the simplest of the three types of photographic lamps shown at right gives the photographer considerable flexibility in choosing the direction and intensity of the illumination. Each lamp operates in a slightly different way, but for portrait lighting, similar principles apply to all.

To begin with, place the light source slightly above and to one side of your subject's face. If you do not have a proper support stand, fix the light to a door, a chair-back or a stepladder, using a spring clamp or heavy adhesive tape.

Unless you are aiming for a particularly harsh effect, you should diffuse the beam of a single lamp. You can do this by bouncing the light from a reflective surface, such as a white umbrella, or by passing it through a translucent screen. Tracing paper or muslin stretched on a wooden frame makes an adequate diffuser. Place the screen a few feet in front of the lamp to keep the diffuser clear of the hot surface of the bulb.

To avoid casting dark shadows on parts of the subject's face, place a reflector on the side that is most distant from the lamp. The larger and closer the reflector is to the subject, the softer and paler the shadows will be.

With tungsten lighting, you can measure exposure by using your camera meter in the normal way, but flash exposures are not so simple to judge. The automatic sensor of a portable flash unit will be misled by the brilliant white surface of a diffuser or reflector, so you must set the unit to manual. Work out a standard setting for your lighting arrangement by running bracketed exposure tests in advance, using wider apertures than for normal flash photographs. An accurate alternative to this procedure is to use a special flash exposure meter.

Sidelighting
For this moody image, the photographer pointed a flash into an umbrella reflector at the side of the subject. A cardboard reflector placed opposite softened shadows on the other side of the face.

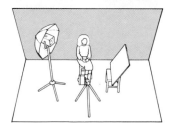

Normal lighting
Here the photographer placed the light at a 45° angle to the subject's face to show more of her features, adjusting the reflector slightly. This is a good arrangement for most portrait photography.

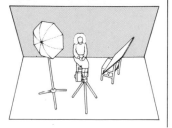

Lighting equipment

A tungsten photolamp (near right) with heatproof reflector is the simplest form of special indoor light. This provides far more light than ordinary bulbs, but you need tungsten-balanced slide film to achieve accurate colors. With a portable flash (center) or powerful studio flash units (far right), you can use film balanced for daylight.

Tungsten photolamp
This gives continuous light so that you can see how the illumination falls on the subject. The type shown is fitted with a reflector dish and a clamp for mounting onto convenient bases.

Portable electronic flash
The strong light from these battery-powered units should be diffused through a screen or bounced off a reflective surface. To preview the effect of the lighting angle, light the scene first with a desk lamp in the position of the flash.

Studio flash
This studio flash unit is fitted with a polished reflector. A built-in tungsten lamp gives continuous light for previewing the lighting effect.

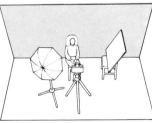

Frontal lighting
Placing the light very close to the camera produces a flatter portrait with greater brilliance. The sitter's eyes reflect the light, and the shadows are small.

Texture and the body

Glamor photographs tend to portray bodies as uniformly even and smooth – and therefore unreal. But human skin – the basis of our whole sense of touch – has textural qualities, and photographs that use light to explore these qualities communicate strongly because they add a new, tactile dimension that moves the image closer to real life.

To show skin texture in sharp detail, strong side-lighting is best. Indoors, the simplest approach is to position the subject so that natural light from a window falls on one side. Alternatively, angle a tungsten photolamp to cast an oblique light on the figure. Often you can reveal interesting textural contrasts by closing in on a selected part of the body. For example, in the picture below, the fuzzy texture of a man's leg and forearm contrasts with the smoothness of his shoulder and torso.

Another way to emphasize texture is to oil or wet the body so that the surface reflects light. Oil has a dramatic, sculptural effect; for this reason, it is more suitable for abstract images. But water gives a delightfully fresh, natural look. And cold water has an invigorating effect, tautening the skin and making it glow alive.

A plain dark background, as in the two pictures on this page, will throw textures into relief. On the other hand, textured surroundings can accentuate the softness and delicacy of skin and hair. You could experiment with thick toweling or a gauzy material indoors. And outdoors the natural textures of sand, wood or rocks, as in the picture opposite, all provide effective contrasts.

A play of water gives movement and light to the supple body above. Gleaming highlights on the ribs contrast with the rounded, shadowed areas of the thigh and hip. Droplets of water accentuate the slightly granular texture of the skin. The model stood under a shower for a picture taken with flash to freeze the drops.

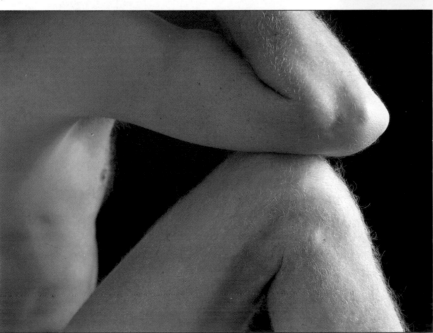

Strong, oblique light picks out the downy hairs covering a man's arm and leg. Softer light on the rest of the body heightens the contrast between smooth, hairless areas and the coarser texture of the skin on the prominent knee and elbow.

A crouching figure within a secluded bowl of rock seems to fit naturally into her surroundings. Rounded contours of weathered sandstone echo the subject's soft curves and set up a subtle contrast between rough and smooth surfaces.

Storm clouds gather over a remote
Canadian farmstead. The bold approach to
composition, with the leaden sky taking
up almost the entire frame, makes the
most of the strange lighting effect. The
long red barn, centered in the frame, is
a strong visual element that helps to
break up the straight line of the horizon.

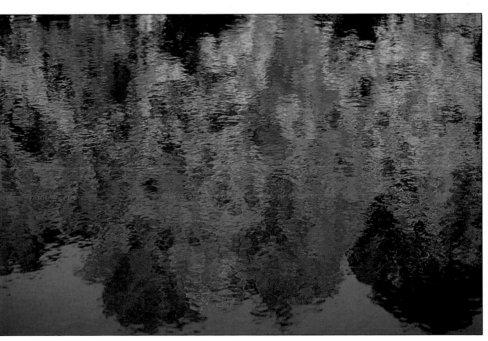

The shimmering reflection of leaves changing color in the fall gives this image the quality of an Impressionist painting. The movement of the sunlit water conveys the rich, glowing colors more effectively than would a more conventional view of the landscape.

Wild poppies *flourish on a patch
of rough ground. The photographer moved
in close with a short telephoto lens to fill
the frame with the small subjects and used
backlighting to intensify the brilliant,
clear colors of the flowers.*

A fallen leaf, coated with frost,
lies caught in a mesh of stiff grass.
The photographer carefully composed the
picture to reveal the intricate patterns
of the tangled grass and the leaf's
structure, traced with silver. He used a
standard lens at its closest focus – $1\frac{1}{2}$ feet.

THE TRAVELING CAMERA

Anticipation is one of the pleasures of travel. And with some advance knowledge of where you are going, you will waste less time and come back with a more interesting photographic record. Also, you will take better pictures if you have packed the right equipment. So before you leave, research the places you will visit, using guides, travel books, brochures and magazines. Such visual material will provide a starting point for your own pictures. You should also find out what kind of weather to expect and the starting times of any special events to be held during your stay. All this research will also help you decide what equipment to take along.

Once you arrive, keep in mind that the best travel photographs convey strongly the character of a place. This is not simply a matter of including some recognizable feature in the viewfinder. An important ingredient is your awareness of being a traveler, of experiencing different light and air, unfamiliar sights, smells and sounds. For a travel picture really to work, it has to capture some of this heightened awareness. Be receptive to the mood of a place and to your own feelings about it. Then look for a telling image or an evocative effect of light, as in the view of Rio de Janeiro opposite, that may express how you feel. Only by finding an individual point of view can you communicate a sense of being in a place.

Rio's famed skyline *challenges the visitor wanting an original view. To get this enchanted cityscape, the photographer waited until twilight, when colorful shimmering lights dramatically set off the city's mountains against the rose-hued sky.*

251

Judging a location

Once you have researched a locale and have a clear idea of the subjects you want to photograph, you should consider the best conditions for taking your pictures. Of course if you are recording an event, timing, and to a certain extent camera position, will be predetermined. But for more stable subjects – scenic views and interesting landmarks or buildings – the time of day and the viewpoint you choose are all-important, as illustrated here.

The first step at any site is to make a reconnaissance visit. If time and the site permit, walk around the subject to assess every possible angle. Make running notes of the advantages and disadvantages of various approaches, and try to imagine how changing lighting conditions will affect each view. Again, postcards of the subject will provide useful comparisons. Deciding when and how to take the picture will depend on what you want to convey about the

Cinderella's Castle in Disneyworld, Florida, forms a backdrop for a colorful parade (above). The photographer chose to concentrate on the holiday atmosphere of the scene, taking the picture in bright light and using a 105 mm telephoto lens to make the castle a prominent subject.

Outlined against the sky at sunset (right), the castle takes on a fittingly fairytale appearance. This picture evokes a romantic mood largely by means of backlighting from a low sun, which has cast warm reflections onto the walls of the castle and the still water beneath.

place, and whether or not you want to include other elements in the composition. For example, the photographer of the picture at left on the opposite page made the castle the setting for a vibrant street parade in brilliant sunshine. The second picture shows a quite different approach: the photographer used the sunset to create a mood of fantasy.

To help you to choose the most effective lighting conditions, find out both the time and the direction of sunrise and sunset; these will depend on the season as well as the place. Remember that the angle and quality of early light change very quickly; arriving at the site even ten minutes late may mean missing the best picture. You may also need to take the weather into account. Where the climate is consistent, you can plan your pictures precisely. Otherwise, be prepared to visit a site several times until conditions are right.

A nighttime view of the floodlit castle (above) produced a contrasty image with a strong theatrical quality. The photographer set a slow shutter speed of 1/60 at f/4 and used the light patterns made by globed streetlights to balance the uniform darkness of the foreground.

In late afternoon, lengthening shadows and oblique, raking light reveal the texture and form of the castle. The selection of a fairly distant camera position encompasses the whole tranquil setting, with the meandering course of the water leading the eye to the subject.

Everyday living

Some of the most fascinating contrasts between one place and another occur at the level of daily life. What is unremarkable to the local people – their work, domestic life and customs – provides a wealth of insights for the visitor, whether traveling in his own country or to more exotic places.

Photographs of people at work reveal much about their culture, as does the picture of Sri Lankan tea-pickers opposite. You must bear in mind that many communities begin the day very early, and you may have to rise at dawn to get the most lively pictures. Photographing the local form of transportation is another good way to convey the flavor of everyday life. Railways have a distinctive character in different countries, and you might frame a traveler in a car window, as in the picture below at left. Religion plays a major and visible role in many countries. The photographer of the Muslim at prayer, below, saw the opportunity for an unusual composition typifying the Islamic way of life.

You do not need any special techniques to obtain such intriguing vignettes: just an acute eye, a willingness to venture off the tourist track, and some discretion. For example, find out if photography is permitted before intruding into a place of prayer and always try to be unobtrusive.

A railway passenger in Kowloon, Hong Kong, gazes pensively from his window seat. The unusual framing produced an image combining the everyday and the exotic.

A Muslim at the Blue Mosque, Istanbul, prostrates himself in prayer. Standing on a step, the photographer pointed downward with a 35mm lens at full aperture.

A string of worry beads casually looped over a man's sun-darkened fingers conveys a ubiquitous facet of life in Greece. The photographer spotted the subject in a café in Corfu and closed in with a 80-200mm zoom lens to frame the hand and the silver beads against the dark background.

Sri Lankan women pick tea on a hill plantation. To emphasize the patterns made by the colorful figures moving along the rows of tea plants with their large back baskets, the photographer chose a vertical format and used a 400mm telephoto lens to compress the perspective.

The original approach

The most fascinating images in a travel portfolio will reveal the photographer's individual interests. What attracts one person may go unnoticed by the next. Wherever you are, make a habit of carefully looking for the distinctive and original aspects of what you see around you.

A detailed approach, isolating just a small part of a scene, is the most effective means of putting your personal stamp on a picture. Frequently, you can frame and dramatize a detail more effectively by using a telephoto or zoom lens than by getting close with a standard lens. You might select a slightly incongruous element, such as the traditional-style clock in modern surroundings, below. Or you could frame a classic subject in a fresh way, as in the picture of the Statue of Liberty, opposite. Finally, remember that you can often make a more interesting picture by enlarging and cropping an image at the printing stage – as demonstrated by the photograph of the woman's capped head below at left.

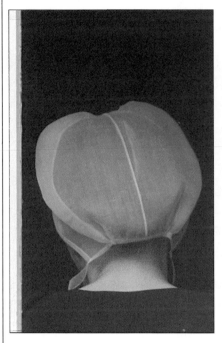

An Amish woman (above) attends Sunday prayer in Lancaster, Pennsylvania. The photographer carefully cropped the detail from a larger image, taken on ISO 400 film – for a soft-toned grainy effect – with a 400mm telephoto lens.

An ornate clock (right) hanging over an insurance building in the City of London bears the company's motto. The photographer used a 300mm lens to throw the geometric lines of modern buildings behind out of focus, obtaining a contrast between old and new, but without clutter.

The head of the Statue of Liberty is tightly framed to make a semi-abstract image. Standing on Liberty Island, the photographer used a 500mm mirror lens to achieve this unusual view.

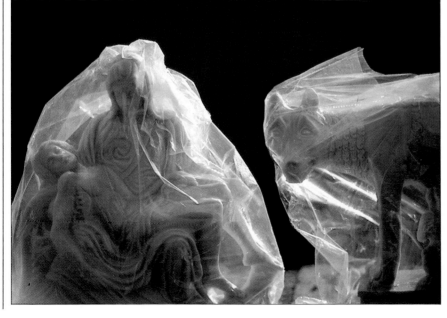

A cowboy's gun in its worn holster caught the photographer's eye in a reconstructed Wild West town in Tombstone, Arizona. A 105mm macro lens filled the frame with the detail.

Replicas on sale in a souvenir booth in Rome (left) invite comparison with their famous originals. The morning light behind the statuettes revealed their details through the transparent plastic.

261

Developing a theme

The pictures on these two pages were all taken in Venice, the city of canals. They show how a single idea or visual element, in this case reflections in water, can lend continuity to travel photographs. By developing such a theme you can also introduce an element of personal interpretation.

Try to decide first what you feel is unique or most significant about a location. Take a little time to explore and get to know your subject. You can combine this process with researching the best views to photograph, but the aim should be to form a general impression. Then look for a way to translate your idea into pictures with a simple visual element that you can repeat and develop – not in every single photograph but in a proportion of them. If your choice of a theme is apt, you will be surprised at the number of visual opportunities it opens up.

Thematic ideas are best kept simple. For example, the coexistence of old and new in a place famous only for its archaeological remains might suggest as a theme pictures of ruins with modern advertising signs deliberately included in the foreground. Other ideas could be the variety of crafts practiced in a location, or the village-like pockets of individuality that survive in some of the biggest and most anonymous cities.

A woman at her housework (above) *seems to waver in the summer heat. In fact, the photograph shows a reflection in the mirror-like surface of a canal on a bright day, with the picture printed upside down. The photographer focused on the reflection with a 105 mm telephoto lens.*

Pedestrians cross a cat-walk (right), *placed over the flooded pavement of St. Mark's Square. A 200 mm lens emphasized the walkers and their reflection, with the bold architecture of the arcade of the Doge's Palace as a backdrop.*

Gondolas stand idle *(left), their distinctive shapes repeated in the misty reflection. The photographer used a 135mm lens to concentrate on the graphic qualities of this detail.*

Ripples of color *(left) fill the whole picture, with no recognizable element to give a clue to the scene's location. Yet this abstract image makes an expressive addition to a series portraying the moods of Venice. The photographer focused an 85mm lens on the surface of the water to catch the shimmering details sharply.*

263

Exotic glimpses

In the West, we are used to photographs that identify people; faces, expressions and clothing give clues to character. The pictures on these pages, all taken in Morocco by Belgian photographer Harry Gruyaert, offer instead tantalizing glimpses of people who are almost entirely hidden from our gaze. In most of the pictures, not only the faces but also the bodies are shrouded. Yet these anonymous, elusive figures exert a powerful presence.

Gruyaert has visited Morocco several times to study the place and its people. The strength of his images arises from his fascination with the country, its customs and the relationships between its people and their surroundings. With the women, he often found himself involved in a game: they were hiding from the camera and provoking it at the same time. The rich colors, the quality of the light, the shadows, the intricate details of the settings: all these were used to place the subjects firmly within their context and to evoke mood and depth. In most of the pictures, a wall provides the background, emphasizing the security of an enclosed world.

Mysterious veiled heads (above) are crisscrossed by shafts of sunlight, the bars of shadow echoing the narrow eye-slits in the women's hoods. Gruyaert set his 35 mm lens at full aperture for this searching close-up view to register the foreground figure slightly out of focus and lead the eye to the figure behind.

A distant figure (above) blends into the pattern of shadows on a sunlit wall. Strong color, texture and shape give greater weight to the foreground of the composition, emphasizing by contrast the elusive, unattainable quality of the figure. The lines of the palm trunks convey depth and provide a natural frame.

A figure in black (left) stands barefoot in the courtyard of a mosque in Fez. The dynamic pattern of the tiles and the stillness of the worshipper create a tension that gives the image tremendous power. The angled, overhead view, framed to include the steep roof, conveys the sense of privacy of an enclosed space.

Dark eyes *are just discernible behind a heavy veil as a passing woman turns to watch the camera (above). The simple shape of the white robes is echoed in the background figures and in the low parapet behind them. Horizontal bands of soft color create a mood of serenity and help give visual unity to the image.*

Marrakesh women *(left) shield their unveiled faces from the camera. Their different reactions produce an intriguing image in which the arrangement of patterns and colors against the rough textured wall at first confuses the eye. To bring out the richness of color and detail, Gruyaert underexposed by one stop.*

The picture essay/1

While single subjects such as local celebrations or styles of dress suit the mini-essay treatment, broader subjects – the life of a region you are exploring, or a city – merit a longer, in-depth approach. And to do justice to the wealth of subject matter, you may need to spend several days working on a theme and finding the best images to express it.

The picture at left and those on the next two pages show how British photographer Michael Freeman approached a detailed photo-essay. His subject is the city of Cartagena, on Colombia's Caribbean seaboard. Freeman wanted to convey something of the city's fascinating history – it was one of the first colonial settlements of the Americas, and the capital of the Spanish Main – as well as its vibrant Latin culture and the tropical setting. Pulling these strands together required a clearly devised plan of action.

The first step was to make a list of topics: views of the setting; architecture old and new; portraits; street life; and activities and events unique to and typical of the place. From this list, Freeman chose subjects that most effectively conveyed the different aspects, taking viewpoints and time of day into account. Because Cartagena is built on several islands, surrounded by marshes and the sea, finding a good vantage point for a clear overview of the city was difficult. To take the scene-setting opener at left, Freeman went to the roof of a modern building in the early evening, used a wide-angle lens and waited until the street lights came on. The next three pictures in the essay, on the following page, provide a contrast between old and new, with different lighting conditions emphasizing the shape or detail of the buildings. Next, two lively images of street life – a Cartagenero playing in a lunchtime band, and examples of local transportation – present a more detailed approach. The essay ends with a very un-citylike picture. But in fact, the fishing scene is strongly typical of the place: such marshy waterways infiltrate Cartagena on all sides.

At twilight, Cartagena's city center twinkles with colored lights. Standing on a prominent rooftop, the photographer waited until just after sunset to get a mixture of natural and artificial light, and took the picture with a wide-angle 20 mm lens for a broad panoramic view.

The picture essay/2

The late afternoon sun brings out the rich colors of the Spanish colonial-style cathedral (right). The photographer used ISO 64 film for good, strong detail, and closed in with a 400mm telephoto lens to record the subject large in the frame.

Modern high-rise buildings on one of Cartagena's islands (below) are softly outlined by the setting sun. From the vantage point of a hill overlooking the island and the bay, the photographer was able to include the shimmering wash of gold on the water and the fringed shapes of palms suggesting a tropical setting.

Tiled roofs and jutting balconies (above) overhang a narrow street in an old quarter of the city. The crosslight from a low sun revealed the textures of the bleached stone walls and rough tiles.

A band musician *plays his saxhorn during a lunchtime performance. Using a 180mm lens, the photographer closed in for a head-and-shoulders portrait of the player, centering the subject in the frame and throwing the surroundings out of focus.*

Gaily decorated local buses *crowd a main street. The photographer chose a high camera position and a diagonal view to convey lively movement in this typical scene, and used a medium telephoto lens to fill the frame with the subjects.*

Fishermen paddle their boat *on a still lagoon at sunrise. Both the subject and time of day form an effective contrast, in mood and color, with preceding images. The photographer used a 400mm telephoto lens at an exposure of 1/125 at f/5.6.*

271

THE NATURAL LANDSCAPE

For photographers, as for painters, landscape holds a lasting appeal. No other subject is so accessible; what we see can be photographed today or tomorrow, in natural light and usually without special equipment. Moreover, the subject seems almost inexhaustible, ranging from the tranquil beauty of fertile woodlands to the stark grandeur of open mountains and deserts.

Yet good landscape photographs are rare. Partly because there are no obvious technical problems, the tendency is to assume that our strong impressions of the scenery will translate themselves onto film effortlessly. The skill of taking landscape pictures lies in understanding how a scene will work photographically instead of just being overwhelmed by the beauty of it all. To compress the sheer scope of a landscape into one image, you need to isolate the visual qualities that will re-create the panoramic view you see or suggest its depth and distance. This section explains some simple techniques that can help you to convey scope, capture natural drama and reveal patterns and textures in ways that will give fresh, original expression to the classic landscape themes.

A still lake mirrors a distant snow-capped peak in the Kluane Game Sanctuary, Yukon, Canada. Framing to show a broad expanse of sky and using a wide-angle lens emphasized a panoramic view.

Viewpoint and scope

Seen from an open viewpoint, the whole landscape appears to spread out in a sweeping panorama. A good photograph of such a scene can re-create for the viewer the same feelings of freedom and exhilaration that originally inspired the photographer.

To evoke these feelings, concentrate attention on the distant horizon and try to strike a harmonious equilibrium between land and sky. This is easiest if you use a wide-angle lens – which naturally takes in a broader view – and compose the image so as to eliminate the foreground, as in the picture at right.

A broken canopy of clouds can help to draw the eye forward across the landscape, as the picture below shows. Point the camera slightly upward so that the horizon does not divide the image into two exactly equal parts.

Even with a standard lens, you can often suggest the openness of landscape by ordering or making a big print and cropping the image at top and bottom, as shown at the bottom of these pages. The use of slow film will help make sure that the enlarged part of the picture does not look too grainy.

Fluffy clouds cast a pattern of shadows on a spread of green fields. A 28mm lens slightly distorted the shape of the clouds, which appear to be moving rapidly toward the distant horizon.

A thicket of silhouetted trees is an interesting composition as it appears in the original picture (above). But by cropping to a horizontal shape, the photographer further strengthened the image. The cropped version, with much of the foreground eliminated, allows the viewer to scan the horizon – as if standing right behind the camera on the side of the darkening hill.

A valley and rolling hills form a
prelude to snow-capped mountains in this
Bolivian landscape. The photographer's
choice of a wide-angle lens and a high
viewpoint has enabled him to convey
powerfully the grandeur of the vast plain.

The marks of man

Many landscape photographers attempt to exclude signs of human habitation or at least play them down. But the pictures here show a more positive response. In all three the landscape is largely natural, but some human element forms a key part of the image: a rough track cuts through an immense wilderness, stone walls thread a hillside with pattern, and a red and white deck chair adds a splash of color in a somber park. The photographers could all have changed viewpoints or lenses to minimize or exclude the human elements, but chose instead to make them cornerstones of the compositions.

Such signs of human activity need to be included with care. You can easily mar landscape pictures by allowing power lines, advertisements, parked cars, roads, or even people to clutter an otherwise unspoiled and natural scene. Keep these elements out of the frame unless you can see a way to use them effectively.

First, carefully study the scene to see if anything at all intrusive appears in the viewfinder. If you spot an unwanted detail, try adjusting the composition. For example, by using a wide-angle lens and moving a foot or two to one side, you may be able to hide the offending detail behind a rock, a tree or the crest of a slope. Narrowing the view with a lens of a longer focal length can also be useful. But if you really want to show untouched landscapes, the best tip is to take pictures early in the morning when there will be fewer cars or people.

A dirt road stretches into the distance across an African plain. By centering on this ribbon of color, the photographer found a bold composition in an almost featureless landscape.

Walled fields surround a lonely English farm. These human creations, framed from a distant slope with a 200mm telephoto lens, made a more interesting picture than the barren hillsides higher up.

A backlit chair stands out brightly amid the dark trees of a city park in the evening. The photographer used a 105 mm lens for a selective view that included the chair as a focal point of the composition.

Exploiting drama

Many landscapes suit a restrained, straightforward style of photography that allows the view to speak for itself without introducing any feeling of camera trickery. But some spectacular landforms or sea-scapes demand special photographic treatment to convey their full drama. Often, the solution is to take the boldest possible approach in lighting, lens choice and viewpoint, as in the pictures here.

With unusual rock shapes, try to show the outline more strongly than anything else. For example, use a telephoto lens to close in and frame the subject tightly, as in the picture at right. Then you could look for a way to silhouette the shapes against the sun, perhaps returning at the right time of day to make this possible. The two pictures on this page show how you can do this either by masking the sun or with the sun very low in the sky.

You can also use the special visual characteristics of lenses with focal lengths of less than 24mm or telephoto lenses with focal lengths of at least 200mm. Very wide-angle lenses distort the appearance of the subject, especially if you tilt the camera. Telephoto lenses compress perspective so dramatically that mountain peaks can be made to loom over foreground crags, as at the top of the opposite page.

Long telephoto lenses also let you take pictures from a greater distance, increasing the number of viewpoints available. For the picture at the bottom of the opposite page, the photographer found that the most dramatic view of the reef islet was from nearby cliffs rather than the much closer beach.

A stone pillar (above), *silhouetted against the setting sun, illustrates the value of returning to a spot at different times of day. At noon the colors were insipid and the column looked dull, but the photographer came back and positioned himself to catch the silhouetted rock just as the sun sank between the pillars.*

A rock arch (left) *stands starkly against the sky in a view with an 18mm lens. To intensify the color to a deep indigo, the photographer used a polarizing filter and cut the exposure by two stops, thus creating an unusually dark and graphic image.*

A distant mountain (above) rises through mist. A 200mm lens brought the mountain closer and gave a sense of scale, while an aperture of f/16 kept the sheer rock and perched bird in focus as a powerful framing device.

White waves (left) wash against a tiny island in this unusual cliff-top view, while the surrounding sea appears almost black. The deliberate underexposure enhanced the feeling of bleakness, and a 200mm lens closed in to accentuate the dizzy feeling of looking down from a height.

283

Trees and forests

Woods and forests form distinctive landscapes in their own right and create complex environments that need different compositional approaches than those required to photograph a single tree.

First, look for a dominant point of interest. In a forest, a view that includes a tangle of branches, a mass of foliage and a variety of vegetation on the ground can easily appear as a disordered jumble. You may have to move around to find a unified image. The photographers who took the pictures shown here all chose different angles of view to convey specific impressions of woodland. The compositions are effective partly because of what they exclude. For example, in the picture below, a close viewpoint crops out the tops of the trees and

details at ground level to concentrate on the trunks and bright patches of sunlit leaves. This is a good approach where the trees grow closely together. For a more distant view, look for a clearing in the trees – a natural glade, a forest creek, or perhaps a firebreak. The photograph at top right captures the mood of a woodland scene even though the trees themselves are secondary to the path that leads the viewer into the frame.

If you cannot find a satisfying view at eye level, one alternative is to point the camera upward and frame the tops of trees. The patterns and colors of leafy branches will stand out strongly against a clear blue sky, particularly the glowing shades of autumn, as in the image at far right.

Dappled shade on a path winding through a carpet of bluebells creates an idyllic woodland scene. Trees leaning inward help to draw the eye to the center and beyond into the inviting distance. To retain detail in the shady areas, the photographer took an exposure reading from the foreground left-hand corner.

Sunlight filtering down to the forest floor (below) throws brilliant highlights on low, leafy branches. The photographer moved round the subject until the light was directly behind, and set a wide aperture to throw the surroundings out of focus.

Autumn leaves blaze with color against a brilliant blue sky. To intensify the contrast and give good color saturation, the photographer used a polarizing filter, which darkened the sky and reduced the flare caused by light reflecting off the shiny leaf surfaces.

Sea and shore

On a calm, overcast day, the sea and wet sand reflect the sky's soft shades of gray and hint at colors that are muted, never brash and brilliant. Often, such cloudy weather seems unpromising for photography. But color film has a remarkable ability to record subtle differences of color. Sometimes this produces scenes tinted with exquisitely delicate hues, particularly at dawn and dusk when sky and sea or sand change through shades of pink and blue, as they do in the picture below. Avoid under-exposure in cloudy conditions, or the sea will look dull and leaden. If anything, a little extra exposure is best, to capture the pastel hues.

Sunlight shows the sea in another mood, picking out deeper, richer colors and touching the breakers with brilliant white crests. On a sunny day, pay special attention to the movement of clouds. When they cross the sun, clouds can throw deep shadows on the sea, producing dark horizons that form a dramatic contrast with the color of sunlit water closer to the shore, as in the image at right. To prevent errors of exposure in such a high-contrast scene, take a meter reading from a midtone – the area between the horizon and the breaking waves in the example shown here.

In blustery weather, you can get good pictures near rocks, where the sea throws up jets of spray, especially if you stand so that the waves are backlit, as in the picture at the bottom of this page. If you can get close enough, a wide-angle lens makes the scene look even more dramatic, but take care that spray does not splash your camera. Wipe away the corrosive salt-water before it dries, and always keep the lens covered with a skylight filter.

A cloudy seascape (left) *turns pink and turquoise as the sun rises. The receding waves left the beach wet, and the photographer used the sheen of the water to mirror the colors of the early-morning sky.*

A wide sea (right) *threatened to soak the photographer when he took this picture, so he moved back from the shore and used a 135mm telephoto lens to frame the waves against the orange light of dusk.*

A white breaker
crashes onto the beach,
adding a froth of white to
the blues of sea and sky.
A polarizing filter helped
make the colors deeper.

Telephoto lenses

When looking at a wildlife subject through a long telephoto lens, one of the most striking things about the image is the shallow depth of field, particularly when the lens is set at a wide aperture. Although the narrow zone of sharp focus may seem to present a problem, in practice you may find it often helps you. Lying in wait, you can conceal yourself and your equipment behind vegetation, and the lens will throw the intervening screen of foliage out of focus, as in the picture at bottom right. With a fixed-aperture mirror lens, used for the picture below, out-of-focus highlights appear as bright discs, known as "doughnuts" – an effect created by the mirror elements within this type of lens, which fold up the light path and thus make the lens more compact.

Shallow depth of field is sometimes also useful to isolate small subjects. For example, in the picture at right, the out-of-focus background draws attention to the birds, despite their relatively small size.

To shift focus with a telephoto lens, you must turn the focusing ring farther than on a standard lens, and an extra second spent focusing can mean a missed picture. With a manual focus telephoto, you can reduce this risk if you keep the lens always set to a point in the middle distance, so that you need to make only small focusing adjustments.

Led by a stag, *kudus splash across a flooded African plain. A 500mm mirror lens picks them out against the light and creates a shimmering wash as highlights in the out-of-focus foreground reproduce as discs – a characteristic effect of this lens. Since the aperture was fixed at f/11 the photographer had to use a fast shutter speed to prevent overexposure.*

A pair of seabirds *perch on a cliff face. The photographer set up his camera on a tripod at the cliff edge, focused carefully on the ledge at a wide aperture and waited until the puffins landed on one of their favourite perches.*

A baby orangutan *waits for its mother, and the photographer's 300mm lens crops tightly in on its anxious expression to make a striking animal portrait taken from a hidden position.*

Birds in flight

When on the ground, birds can seem ungainly and awkward; their true grace and beauty emerge only in flight. Try to take pictures when the birds are close enough to fill a good area of the viewfinder frame. If you are using a telephoto lens, large species such as herons, storks and pelicans present good subjects, even at a height. But often the best moments to capture birds are when they are taking off or landing, particularly if you can include a reflection in the frame, as in the picture at top right.

Focusing manually on a speeding subject can present problems even for the most experienced photographer, though most modern autofocus cameras are able to keep up. Many species of birds hover steadily on thermals and updrafts. For example, seagulls tend to follow boats at a fixed distance, so that framing and focusing are easy as the birds spread their wings to catch the rising air.

For a bird flying toward the camera, preset the focus and press the shutter release when the bird begins to look almost sharp. If you are using an autofocus camera, select either continuous focus or predictive focus.

When the direction of flight is past the camera, you should pan to follow the birds, as the photographer did for the picture at right center. Birds usually follow a fixed route when leaving or returning to a nest, so you may get several chances to take the same picture.

A heron takes flight
and a 300 mm lens isolates
the elegant outline against
the surface of the water.
Laboring to gain height,
the bird was slow enough
to allow the photographer
to take several pictures.

Soaring seagulls (below)
present an easy target as
they hover above the deck
rail of the boat on which the
photographer was standing.
They were so close that even
with a standard lens the
birds appear sufficiently
big to dominate the picture.

Speeding birds flash past
the camera, their outlines
blurred by a shutter
speed of 1/15. The result
is an image that sums up the
magic of flight.

A tern (below) wheels
around a high cliff top.
The photographer preset
the focusing ring on the
300 mm lens and took a
series of pictures as birds
from a flock flew into
the plane of sharp focus.

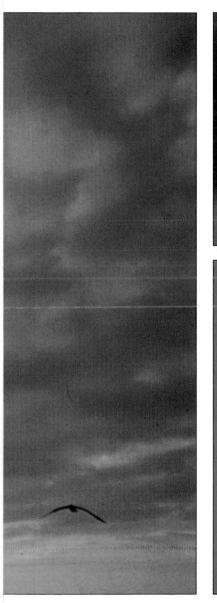

Wildlife with flash

Many animals – mammals in particular – become active only as night falls. Nature pictures taken with flash at night have a special vividness, perhaps because they show us a world of hidden activity.

Nocturnal animals can see in the dark much better than humans. Nevertheless, if you give your eyes 20 minutes or so to adapt to the darkness, you will find that they become more sensitive, particularly to movement at the periphery of your vision. To stalk animals at night, you must be aware of everything around you and not look fixedly ahead.

If the night is black, carry a flashlight with a cardboard snoot that narrows the beam. Far from causing alarm, a bright light often mesmerizes animals and may pick up the telltale twin reflections of their eyes, giving you a useful guide to focusing. However, the best chance of getting pictures such as the one of the badger on the opposite page is to wait patiently in a suitable camera position and use a remote release if necessary.

Unless the subject is very close to the camera, use the most powerful flash you can. Outdoors, with no reflective surfaces, the light loses intensity quickly, so you should first check what range your unit provides by making some test exposures at different distances. Even with a powerful flash, you may need to use a fast film of ISO 400 or ISO 1000 for subjects more than a few feet away.

Flash is useful during the day also if you want to freeze fast-moving subjects; the picture of a hovering hummingbird below shows just how fast flash can be. However, the unit must be close to the subject so that the burst of light is very short and bright enough to overpower the daylight.

A tiny hummingbird sips nectar from a flower, its wing beats frozen by twin automatic flash units. Despite the very brief flash duration (1/10,000) the bird's wing tips are still slightly blurred. The photographer placed the camera on a tripod, as shown below, and used a 100mm macro lens at f/11.

Flash equipment
For tiny subjects, such as the bird in the picture above, flash units like the one at left provide ample power. In addition, their exposure-regulating circuits provide a useful way to control flash duration, as they curtail the flash quickly when the subject is close to the flash unit. To soften harsh shadows or to create more even lighting, it is possible to link two or more flash units with a cable, as here, or to trigger them with a remote control device.

*A **badger*** *emerges from hiding, and a flash unit illuminates it brilliantly. The photographer located the den by day, and set up the camera and flash while there was still enough light to focus. He used a tripod to support the motor-driven camera, and attached the flash unit to a stand as diagrammed at right. When the animal appeared, the photographer triggered the camera and flash with a remote release.*

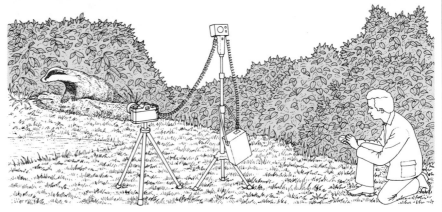

Animals at the zoo

The time of day is almost as important in zoo photography as in the wild. To get effective pictures like that of the romping polar bear at the bottom of this page, you need to be on hand at feeding times or else arrive when the zoo opens and the animals tend to be more active.

There are some simple ways to make the animals' surroundings as well as their behavior look as natural as possible. Modern zoos that use moats and ditches rather than bars make it possible to screen out all surroundings except those that suggest the animals' natural habitat. One effective technique is to close in on the subjects as tightly as possible with a telephoto lens. You could even consider showing just a detail – an approach that works well for subjects that have strong color markings, such as the toucan below.

By walking around the subject, you may be able to find a camera angle that allows you to use lighting to hide evidence of an artificial environment. For example, in the polar bear picture, backlighting in bright sunlight has thrown into deep shadow the masonry walls at the back of the pool. And by aiming up high into the light, the photographer of the monkeys at the bottom of the opposite page suggested a jungle setting.

A toucan's bright bib of yellow feathers forms a marked contrast to the deep black of the majority of its plumage. The photographer set his zoom lens to its maximum focal length of 200 mm to frame the bird's head, bill and breast. At this focal length, the bars of the bird's enclosure blurred out.

A polar bear splashing in its pool is caught by a fast shutter speed of 1/1000. The photographer took up his position across a moat just before feeding time, when the animal's impatience ensured a lively action picture.

A green snake coiled on a branch makes an effective image. The photographer noticed the snake in a reptile house and chose an angle that would suggest a natural-looking background. A wide aperture helped to throw out of focus a concrete wall behind the branches.

A pair of zoo monkeys chatter on a high branch in the Monkey Jungle near Miami. To avoid recording people and paths in the background, the photographer aimed up at the sky. He allowed an extra stop-and-a-half exposure so that the monkeys would not appear as silhouettes.

Flowers/1

Wildflowers can splash patches of bright, often startling, color across otherwise bare landscapes or form brilliant contrasts with the subdued browns and greens of foliage and trees. To make the most of such contrasts, try to relate the flowers to their surroundings. One way to do this is to select a viewpoint low to the ground and quite close to the plant, as the photographer did when taking the striking picture below.

For maximum depth of field, stop the lens down to a small aperture and use the camera's depth-of-field preview control to check that both flower and background are in sharp focus. If the flowers are sheltered, you may be able to balance a very small aperture by using a slow shutter speed, with the camera on a tripod or other support.

An alternative to this kind of richly detailed image is to throw foreground flowers out of focus so that only their intense colors catch the eye. Use a telephoto lens set at a wide aperture and focus on the background. In the picture at right, a mirror lens has spread the flower heads into blobs of color, almost as if dropped from a full paint brush, creating a picture that has far more impact and immediacy than one designed to record the flowers accurately, as a recognizable species.

Red and yellow flowers (right) contrast with the dull olives of woodland. A 500mm mirror lens produced a shimmering effect in the foreground flowers and in the equally out-of-focus background highlights. Such lenses save weight when you go walking, being much lighter than telephoto lenses of the equivalent focal length.

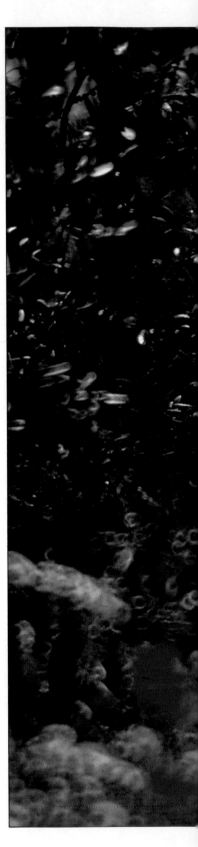

Claret-cup cacti (left) thrive on a barren crag above a valley in Big Bend National Park, Texas. To keep both parts of the picture in focus, the photographer used an aperture of f/16. The bright sunshine enabled him to set a shutter speed fast enough to stop the wind-blown blossoms from blurring.

EXTENDING YOUR RANGE

Anyone who has mastered the basic skills of photography and seeks further challenges is in an enviable position. It would take a lifetime to exhaust all the possible ways of creating photographic images. And whatever your special interests, there will inevitably be a way of extending them into the realm of advanced image making. For example, if you want to capture the exuberant vitality of an athlete in motion or of children at play, you are likely to find the split-second timing of action photography highly rewarding. At the other extreme, if your interests run toward taking professionally lit portraits or fashioning carefully composed still-lifes, like the one shown opposite, you will no doubt delight in the enormous control that you gain over a picture's appearance as you learn to use studio techniques.

Action photography and studio techniques are only two of the subjects explored in this last part of the book. There is also a section demonstrating some simple methods you can use to create dramatic special effects. And another section describes how you can use adverse weather and tricky lighting conditions to produce striking imagery. In the two concluding sections, you will see how to develop and print your pictures and how to present the best of them in slide shows and albums or as framed prints. The representative sampling of pictures on the following pages shows the immensely varied results that these advanced techniques can produce with a bit of diligence and imagination.

A wriggle of light twists around a wooden knob and a feather, and rises behind them in a bold crescent to create a cool still-life with a hint of Oriental imagery. Light shining through a cardboard cutout was responsible for the main crescent, while a curved acrylic sheet created the compressed reflections of the crescent and knob at the bottom.

Fencing's elegance *is captured (above) in a spectral image. A slow shutter of 1/8 had the effect of dissolving the figures' swift motions against the dark backdrop.*

The graceful arc of a
gymnast's legs slicing the
air (right) appears in
consecutive images by means
of a stroboscopic flash unit
firing rapid flashes. The
continuous illumination from
overhead stadium lights
picks up a sweeping amber
trace. The gymnast's iron
stillness and the multiple
images of his legs suggest
both speed and control.

Swimmers launch their bodies toward the water at the start of a race. Arched backs generate a sense of powerful propulsion, and the eel-like limbs, crammed into the frame by a telephoto lens, are stopped with a shutter speed of 1/1000.

Sweat and water spray
from the contorted face of
Larry Holmes as he ends a
punishing sparring session
in preparation for a world
heavyweight title defense.
The ringside photographer
closed in and used flash
to freeze the droplets.

A motorcycle racer banks over to take a corner, the bright red of the rider's suit standing out against the dark of the track. The photographer used a special prism filter to create the repeated image that gives such a dramatic impression of high speed.

A plastic sandal and a bulb of garlic (below), faintly reflected in the sheet of red acrylic they stand on, make a memorable still-life with visually strong contrasts of color, form and texture, and of organic and man-made materials. The light source was a diffused photolamp angled onto the subjects from above. The lamp produced a reflected highlight on the toe of the sandal, the focal point of the composition.

A glass of carbonated mineral water (right), containing an ice cube, a slice of lemon and a cherry, fills the frame with an image of thirst-quenching refreshment. A portable flash unit, aimed at a reflector immediately behind the glass, was quite adequate to light this small subject, and the burst of light was brief enough to freeze the motion of the tiny bubbles.

Unearthly blue light and deep shadows (left) impart a macabre air to a portrait. The photograph was taken on tungsten-balanced film, with the subject lit from below by daylight-balanced fluorescent tube lighting. The closeness of the light source washed out part of the image, imparting a sense of the supernatural.

A silhouetted profile (right) blends naturally into a starlit seascape. Four elements in combination make up the image. To obtain the silhouette, the photographer posed the woman against a white background, lit only the background and used a blue filter over the lens. Tiny holes pierced in black cardboard produced an image of twinkling stars. After sandwiching this with the silhouette, the photographer copied the sandwich onto a sheet of film masked off at the bottom. With the top masked in turn, a second exposure recorded the sea. Finally, the photographer copied a slide of the moon onto the same piece of film, exposing the sky area alone.

The action around us

The great advantage of ordinary action situations is their accessibility. You can study a scene at your leisure, look for good subjects, try out different viewpoints and return later if the light is poor.

Essentially there are two approaches you can take with everyday action photography. You can go to a promising location, such as a busy street, and snatch the action as it happens, or you can plan a particular photograph. The picture of motorcyclists on the opposite page was set up in advance: the photographer fixed his camera to the back of a car and waited until the bikes were just a few feet away before triggering the shutter.

Anticipation is also important with a more spontaneous approach. Evaluate the setting and decide how you want to portray the subject. The two pictures at right and far right here show figures in motion, and both were taken with a telephoto lens – but the results are very different. For the roller-skaters, the photographer closed in to make the subjects fill the frame and threw the distracting background out of focus. The figure on the beach is more abstract, and the long lens has been used to bring the background closer. In some situations, you can predict what will happen and preset your camera so that you are ready to catch the moment of action. The picture below is an example: two children were playing with a hose, and sooner or later, one was bound to turn the water on his friend.

Rollerskate novices (*above*) *have a go. A 300mm lens at maximum aperture enabled the photographer to close in and catch the mingled excitement and uncertainty, while reducing the color and movement in the background to a soft blur.*

A boy's face (*left*) *registers the shock of an unexpected shower. The photographer preset the focus and an exposure of 1/125 at f/5.6 and then just waited for the fun to start.*

An early morning bather
(above) *prepares to plunge*
into the surf. A 300 mm lens
has compressed perspective
so that the mountains and
ships seem nearer and form
a backdrop to the figure.

Two motorcycles (right)
seem to bear down on the
viewer at dizzying speed.
The photographer attached
the camera to the tail of a
car – driven ahead of the bikes
by a friend – and operated
the shutter with a cable
release from the back seat.
A 15 mm wide-angle lens gave
broad coverage and good
depth of field, while a shutter
speed of 1/125 streaked
the background.

Fast shutter

Action photography calls for a camera with a top shutter speed of at least 1/1000. Some modern cameras are even faster – as quick as 1/8000, or even 1/12,000. But must you use your camera's fastest speed to freeze action, or will a slower speed be sufficient?

The answer obviously depends on how fast your subject is moving, but other factors are important too. For example, the world's fastest sprinter reaches a speed of about 27 miles per hour, and in the course of an exposure lasting 1/1000, his body will have moved forward about half an inch. If you are photographing a whole field of six or eight runners from some distance with a standard lens, then body movement of half an inch is unlikely to be significant, and the picture will look sharp. But if you choose to close in with a powerful telephoto lens and show the strain on the face of the leading runner as he crosses the finishing line, a half-inch movement could make the magnified winner's profile look blurred and indistinct.

In sporting events such as auto racing, in which speeds are many times faster than on a running track, the direction of movement has an even greater bearing on the sharpness. If the subject is moving directly toward or away from the camera, the image in the viewfinder does not move across the frame. Instead, it simply appears to get bigger or smaller, and to arrest this slight change you can use shutter speeds that would be too slow to freeze the same subject passing across the frame, as demonstrated in the sequence below at left.

The chart below at right offers a rough guide to the relative shutter speeds at which you should be able to freeze different kinds of movement. But bear in mind that a host of factors can affect sharpness, including the focal length of your lens and your distance from the subject. You should use these speeds experimentally, and combine them with swinging the camera around to follow the subject – the panning technique explained in detail on pages 346-47.

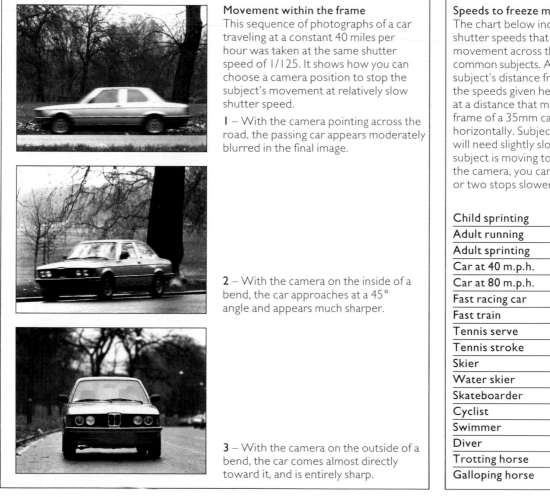

Movement within the frame
This sequence of photographs of a car traveling at a constant 40 miles per hour was taken at the same shutter speed of 1/125. It shows how you can choose a camera position to stop the subject's movement at relatively slow shutter speed.

1 – With the camera pointing across the road, the passing car appears moderately blurred in the final image.

2 – With the camera on the inside of a bend, the car approaches at a 45° angle and appears much sharper.

3 – With the camera on the outside of a bend, the car comes almost directly toward it, and is entirely sharp.

Speeds to freeze movement
The chart below indicates the slowest shutter speeds that will stop the movement across the frame of some common subjects. A lot depends on the subject's distance from the camera – the speeds given here are for subjects at a distance that makes them fill the frame of a 35mm camera, held horizontally. Subjects farther away will need slightly slower speeds. If the subject is moving toward or away from the camera, you can allow a speed one or two stops slower than is indicated.

Child sprinting	1/250
Adult running	1/250
Adult sprinting	1/500
Car at 40 m.p.h.	1/500
Car at 80 m.p.h.	1/1000
Fast racing car	1/2000
Fast train	1/1000
Tennis serve	1/1000
Tennis stroke	1/500
Skier	1/1000
Water skier	1/500
Skateboarder	1/500
Cyclist	1/500
Swimmer	1/125
Diver	1/1000
Trotting horse	1/250
Galloping horse	1/1000

Fast film

Shutter speeds fast enough to freeze rapid action dramatically reduce the amount of light that gets to the film. One solution – often the only one – is to use faster film, as outlined in the table at right.

To freeze the action of the circus performer below, the photographer had to use a shutter speed of 1/500. With a medium-speed film, the dim lighting of the big top would have forced him to use an aperture of f/1.8 – impractical because his lens had a maximum aperture of f/4. Loading the camera with ISO 400 film enabled him to capture the scene with the f/4 aperture.

In exceptionally bad light, even the fastest film may not be sufficiently sensitive. But by increasing the development time of color slide or black-and-white film during processing – a technique called pushing the film – you may be able to wring out a little extra speed. To use this technique – illustrated at the bottom of the opposite page – you set the camera's film speed dial at one or two stops above the ISO rating of the film you are using. Then, when you send the film to a laboratory, ask the processor to increase development equivalently.

The availability of fast film
The 35mm format offers the broadest range of fast films, though medium format 120 rollfilm also comes in a wide selection of fast speeds.

Color prints

The fastest color print film has a speed of ISO 3200. This is available in 120 and 35mm formats. However, most film manufacturers limit their fastest color print film to ISO 1600.

Color slides

The fastest 35mm color slide film has a speed of ISO 1600. In the 120 format, the top speed is ISO 1000, though pushing the film increases this to ISO 2000 (see box opposite below).

Black-and-white

Black-and-white film has speeds up to ISO 3200 in the 35mm format, but the limit in the 120 format is ISO 400. Pushing the films can double or even treble their effective speeds.

A human canonball speeds toward the safety net. The photographer used a 200mm lens from a normal seat in the circus tent, with fast ISO 400 film.

At a harness race, rapidly fading sunlight casts a warm glow on a horse and driver. Only by using a film with a speed of ISO 400 was the photographer able to catch a sharp image (1/250 at f /2.8, 135mm lens).

Pushing film

For the sequence below, the photographer progressively uprated the film speed to achieve faster shutter speeds and less blur, thus effectively underexposing. The processor then "pushed" the film's development time to compensate.

Developed normally, ISO 400 film has good color, but dim light forced the photographer to use a speed of 1/60, so movement has blurred the picture.

Uprating the film one stop (to 800), gives a speed of 1/125, which records a sharper image. But longer development boosts grain and dulls color.

Pushing film too far can cut image quality. Here, a three stop push gives a speed of 1/500, but grain size and color are unacceptable.

Prefocusing

The furious pace of much action photography means that maintaining sharp focus at all times is extremely difficult – some subjects move so rapidly that even the most up-to-date autofocus cameras struggle to keep up with the action.

With autofocus cameras, the problem is not the focusing itself, but the short delay while the camera evaluates sharpness, and moves the lens elements to the right position. If you are using an autofocus lens that has a focus-limiting device, you can use this to reduce the delay, as explained below at right. Otherwise, try panning with the subject as it passes.

You may alternatively wish to focus manually, and prefocus the lens. You determine where the best of the action is likely to happen, focus on that spot, wait for the subject to reach it, and then release the shutter.

The most critical judgement is timing. Press the shutter release a fraction too soon or too late, and the subject will be out of focus. The trick is to anticipate the moment at which the subject will reach the point of focus, and shoot a fraction of a second before. For your first attempts, try prefocusing on a fixed, well-defined area. Take the example of a horse clearing a jump at left below. You can prefocus on the top rail in the knowledge that the animal must pass that spot. Having focused, wait until the horse's leading foreleg has just crossed the bar – then shoot. This allows for your reaction time, and for the time taken by the camera's mirror to flip out of the way of the film, giving you a perfectly focused image.

Some autofocus SLRs have a trap focus mode which automatically releases the shutter at the right moment. You prefocus the lens, and the camera fires the shutter the moment a subject enters the autofocus frame at the same distance from the camera as the plane of sharp focus.

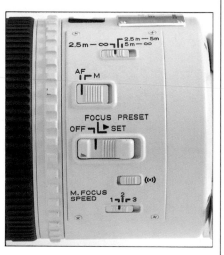

Focus-limiting devices
The newest autofocus lenses adjust focus very rapidly indeed, but there is still a significant time-lag while the lens "hunts" for the subject. The delay is longest when the lens has to make large changes in focus. To solve this problem, some lenses have a switch that limits the travel of the focusing mechanism. For example, the lens shown above can be set to "hunt" only in the range 5m-∞. By switching to this setting when photographing distant subjects, you will greatly reduce the camera's response time.

A horse and rider are stopped in mid-jump. The fence rails provided the photographer with an ideal prefocusing spot. As soon as the forelegs came into focus, he pressed the shutter release.

Panning

By following a moving subject across the frame with your camera during exposure, you effectively reduce the rate of movement. Panning, as this technique is called, enables you to use a relatively slow shutter speed to stop action, while creating background blur to help suggest movement.

In some areas of high-speed photography, panning is essential if you want a sharp image of the subject. With a static camera position, even a shutter speed of 1/8000 may not be fast enough to freeze a racing car or motorcycle traveling across the frame close to you. But by panning you can obtain the kind of crisp image illustrated at the bottom of this page. In an absolutely sharp panned picture the speed of the subject relative to the movement of the camera during the exposure is zero. By slowing the shutter speed and the speed of the panning movement, you can blur or streak the subject. Against a colorful background, slight blurring can suggest a whirling velocity, as in the photograph at right.

Whatever the subject and shutter speed, the basic object of panning is to achieve a smooth, continuous movement of the camera. Start by assessing in advance the course that the subject will take, and prefocus on the spot at which you estimate the subject will pass closest to you. Stand facing this spot with your shoulders parallel to the subject's line, and set a shutter speed of around 1/60 or 1/125, depending on the subject's speed. As the subject approaches, without moving your feet, swivel your hips round to pick it up in the viewfinder. Keep the subject in the center of the frame until it is almost directly in front of you and then press the shutter release. Remember to follow through smoothly after the exposure to avoid any image distortion.

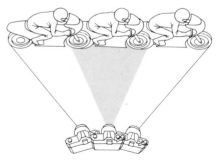

Accurate panning, *as diagrammed above, froze the movement of the racing motorcycle at left. The photographer selected a shutter speed of 1/1000 and pressed the shutter release in the middle of the swiveling motion plotted in the diagram. This ensured a sharp image in the exact center of the frame.*

Horses racing across a field convey the joy of free movement. Fast panning at 1/60 recorded the main subject's head and shoulders crisply: but the galloping hooves, the other horses and the verdant surroundings have streaked and blurred.

Polo ponies, photographed at two different shutter speeds, show how the effects of panning can be controlled. The photographer set a shutter speed of 1/8 for the picture at left in order to creatively mask all detail. At 1/125, panning has stopped the pony – but has only just blurred the background.

Track and field

The most important factor in deciding how you should photograph a running race is the length of the course. An approach that produces good pictures of a sprint will not necessarily work well if you apply it to a marathon.

Short track races last just seconds, and you may have time to take only one picture. At such events, decide which part of the race you most want to photograph, and concentrate on capturing this one moment. For example, in the picture at right, the photographer chose to show the runners accelerating just after the starting pistol was fired.

Middle-distance races of course last longer than sprints and, if you can move freely around the track, you may be able to get pictures of both start and finish. However, if you are confined to a single place, perhaps a seat in the stands, try to be close to the finish, or overlooking the final bend where the runners put on a last effort to gain the lead.

Marathons and other long races have rather different action peaks for the photographer. The massed start makes a dramatic contrast with the finish, where the leading runner may cross the line while the rest of the field is out of sight. The miles that separate start and finish give ample opportunity for portraying the isolation and exhaustion of individual runners, although the finish can provide particularly poignant moments – as at right below.

Four sprinters (above) surge forward at the start of a 100 meter race. Looking down the track from an ordinary seat in the stands, the photographer prefocused a 200mm lens on a selected group, with a speed of 1/1000 to fix their burst of energy in motionless symmetry.

A lone runner (left) crosses a hill during a cross-country race. By using a 400mm lens, the photographer isolated him against the backdrop of a distant valley.

An exhausted winner (left) hits the tape at the end of a road race. Free public access to the finish line meant that a 135mm lens was sufficient to fill the frame with a close-cropped image of the victor.

Winter sports

To catch the exhilaration of winter sports, you must first adjust your photographic techniques to compensate for the low temperatures, and for the glare of snow or ice.

Exposure control needs special attention in snow-covered settings. An SLR's through-the-lens meter will indicate a reduced exposure to deal with the large expanse of white, and to retain a brilliant whiteness you should increase the metered exposure by between one and two stops. Remember to revert to normal exposure settings for pictures such as the one at bottom right, in which the sky rather than the snow forms the background.

On a sunny day, the areas of snow in shade reflect the color of the sky, so they look blue on film.

Provided that other parts of the picture are sunlit, these blue shadows look quite natural, as can be seen from the image below. But if the entire scene is in the shade, you should use a No. 85C orange filter.

In cold weather, you need to take extra care of your camera. Keep it warm under your coat between exposures, because the batteries that power the meter, and possibly also the shutter, provide less current when they get cold. When you finish taking pictures, wrap your camera in a plastic bag before taking it indoors. Otherwise, moisture may condense on the cold surfaces, and damage the camera's mechanism. In extremely cold conditions, bare skin sticks to exposed bare-metal parts of camera and lens, so cover these with tape.

Laughing and tumbling, a crowd of friends enjoy the year's first snow. The photographer pointed down from a high bank to provide a uniform background that focused attention on the colors and swirling action.

Flying through the air, a ski hotdogger judges her landing. A polarizing filter darkened the blue sky, and a shutter speed of 1/1000 caught a sharp picture of the flurry of snow.

Speeding downhill, a skier turns to follow the trail. To prevent the snow from looking a featureless white, the photographer waited until late in the afternoon, when a low sun emphasized each hillock and picked out the tracks of earlier skiers.

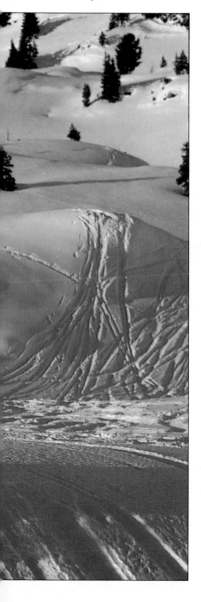

353

On the water

Water is a superb indicator of speed and movement. With activities that take place on the surface – waterskiing, surfing and windsurfing – you can use the flying spray and the foaming wake to convey the invigorating excitement of the action.

Like snow and ice, water reflects a great deal of light, especially spray or a breaking wave. Usually, you will need to open up at least half a stop to avoid underexposing your subject. Surfing, windsurfing and waterskiing usually take place some way from the shore, so you will need a long telephoto lens to close in on the subject if you are standing on the beach. The ideal position for taking waterskiing pictures is from the back of the towing boat. The skier's distance from the boat remains constant, so focusing is easy. A 300mm lens will enable you to frame the skier tightly. But you might instead concentrate on the wall of spray sent up by the skis, and keep the figure itself quite small. This approach is equally effective from the shore, and if you photograph at dusk you can obtain truly dramatic effects, as in the picture opposite.

A vantage point on a rocky headland can bring you close to surfboarders or windsurfers, but these two subjects present spectacular images even from a distance, as the photograph below demonstrates. With windsurfing, the camera angle is particularly important; the best pictures show the subject either backlit or, as here, heading toward the camera so that both the sail and the windsurfer are visible.

A waterskier skims the surface of a lake at dusk. A shutter speed of 1/1000 at f/5.6 with ISO 200 film froze the backlit subject and the curtain of spray behind.

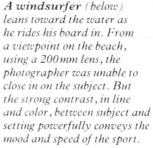

A windsurfer (below) leans toward the water as he rides his board in. From a viewpoint on the beach, using a 200mm lens, the photographer was unable to close in on the subject. But the strong contrast, in line and color, between subject and setting powerfully conveys the mood and speed of the sport.

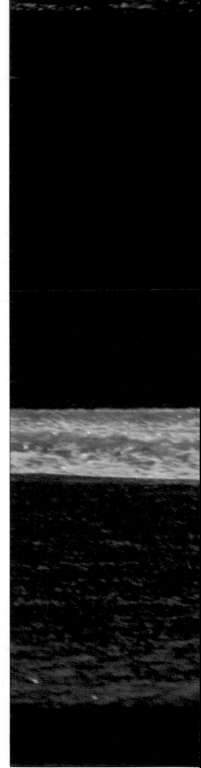

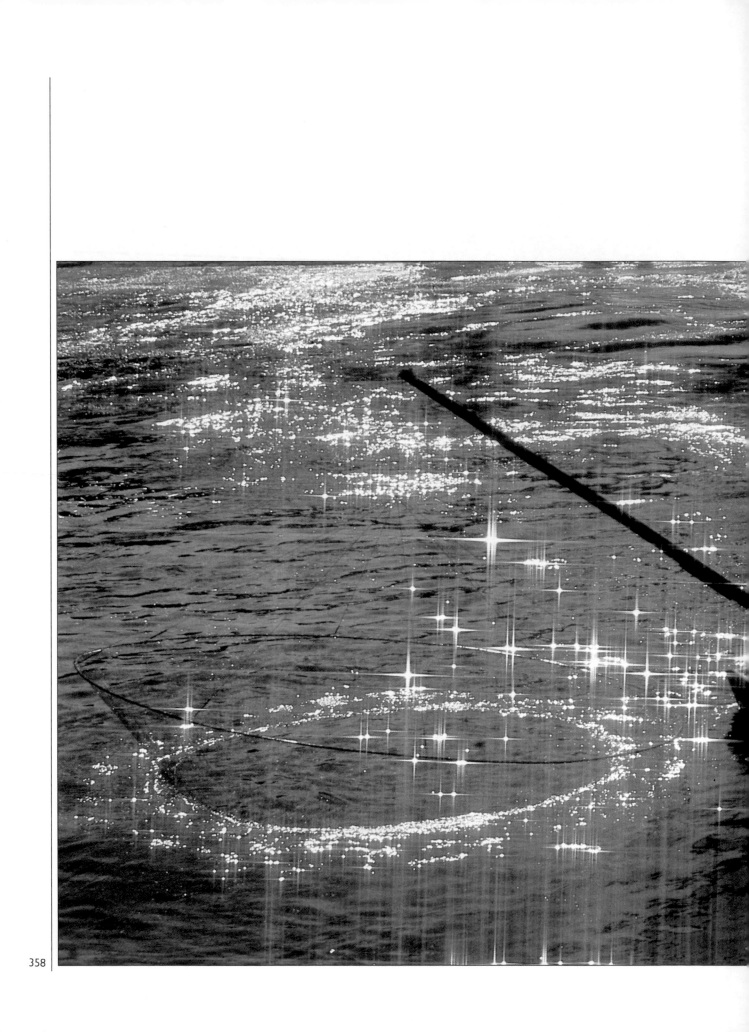

CREATING SPECIAL EFFECTS

Many photographers are content with the realistic pictures that reproduce the world as we perceive it. And because we are accustomed to such photographs, when the camera does create illusions the results are all the more striking. Taking reality as a starting point, these images surprise us with their weird juxtapositions or spin beautiful images with unearthly forms and colors.

This section introduces the fascinating world of special effects photography and explains some of the basic effects that you can exploit to make memorable surrealistic images. None of the techniques is beyond the reach of the amateur. For many, the only requirement is a willingness to experiment freely with ordinary equipment and film. Others require a little more in the way of camera attachments, like the relatively inexpensive filter that added glittering highlights to the view of a lake at left.

The basic techniques covered here should stimulate further exploration. Learn to break the rules uninhibitedly. And do not worry if the results are unpredictable – this is all part of the pleasure of special effects photography.

Two fishermen winch their net out of a lake to inspect their catch by the light of the early evening sun. A starburst filter over the lens turned the reflected highlights into a pattern of four-pointed stars.

Tricks with a slow shutter

The deliberate choice of a shutter speed that is too slow to stop a subject's movement can produce exciting and original pictures. Depending on the direction and speed of the subject, you can convey movement with slight blurring while still recording a recognizable image, as in the photograph of the flag below. Or you can create strange effects such as those in the picture on the opposite page, below, in which the central part of the image has dissolved into a formless blur.

To stop camera shake during slow shutter-speed exposures, you usually need to use a tripod. If you are photographing in daylight or bright light, you may also need to put a neutral density filter over your lens to compensate for the slower shutter speed: a 0.9 filter, for example, reduces the light reaching the film by three stops. Neutral density filters also enable you to set a wider aperture for shallow depth of field, so that you can throw a distracting background out of focus.

You can obtain beautiful abstract images by using a very slow shutter, of several seconds or more, for dusk scenes with colored lights. During lengthy exposures, even slight movement of the subject will cause highlights to spread into shadow areas and colors to flow. In the lower picture opposite, the effect was exaggerated by shining a colored light onto the subject. The reinforced glass of the balcony diffused the hues of the street lights below, adding texture to the composition.

A flag fluttering in the breeze appears as soft ripples of color at a slow shutter speed of 1/8 second. The photographer carefully framed the composition to include the tones and lines of the wall behind, which echo those of the flag.

Whirling chairs at a fairground dissolve into smoky shapes resembling the dark clouds behind them. A 1/4 second exposure also streaked the lights but recorded the rest of the scene sharply.

A wind-blown sheet on a line glows with vivid, fluorescent color against a cool twilight setting. The photographer shined a red lamp on the sheet and set a five-second exposure to get the diaphanous effect against the soft background hues.

Tricks with flash

With a little ingenuity and technical know-how, an electronic flash unit can be used to create exciting and unusual images – as these pictures show.

The easiest way to do this is to take pictures in dim light at a slow shutter speed – between 1/15 and one full second. When you press the shutter release, the flash fires but the shutter remains open, so that the ambient light continues to form an image. If the background is lit continuously from another source, a moving subject lit momentarily by flash will appear sharp but ghostlike, as on the opposite page below.

Some dedicated flash units, and the built-in flash units on many modern compact cameras, can balance the flash and ambient light levels automatically – this is often referred to as slow synch fill-in flash. However, this technique may not work when your SLR camera is set to program mode. On some SLRs, the slowest shutter speed the program will set on flash exposures is 1/60, which results in a brightly lit subject and a dark background. To solve the problem, switch to shutter priority mode or manual exposure mode.

A few, top-of-the-range flash units offer a second curtain synch option (sometimes known as rear curtain synch). Normally, the flash fires when the first shutter curtain opens fully, but when second curtain synch is set, the flash fires moments before the second shutter curtain starts to move. This has the advantage that the flash freezes a moving subject at the end of the exposure, rather than at the beginning, so trails of ambient light appear to follow the subject, giving a far more realistic effect.

If you have a tripod, you can produce interesting pictures by firing the flash several times on a moving subject, during a single exposure. This technique is known as multiple flash and is explained opposite. Similar, but more dynamic effects can be achieved using stroboscopic flash. In stroboscopic mode, a flash unit fires several, brief bursts of flash in quick succession. These record even fast moving subjects as a series of separate images on a single frame.

Another useful technique is to fit colored filters, or stretch brightly colored material, over the flash head. The photographer who took the picture on the opposite page, below, used the red cellophane wrapper from a candy bar to add brilliant color to the foreground.

A roller skater speeds backward past the camera, his motion frozen by a flash. By panning to follow the figure during the one-second exposure, the photographer spread the lights around him into brilliant streaks of color.

Multiple flash

In darkness, you can make several flash exposures on one frame. For multiple images of a single subject, attach the camera to a tripod, and lock the shutter open using the B setting and a lockable cable release. Then fire the flash to light the subject in several positions. For the example at left, the model moved away from the camera and the photographer followed her, firing a flash at each of three locations, as diagrammed below.

A splash of red from a filtered flash breaks the monotony of blank gray city slabs. A passer-by, frozen in motion by the flash, looks like an apparition, because the floodlit wall behind her formed an image on film during the 15-second exposure.

Filters for simple effects/1

By skillfully using filters to alter the color and quality of light, you can manipulate the mood of an image without making it obvious that a special effect is involved. The pictures on these pages owe their distinctive sense of atmosphere to the subtlety with which filters were used to support the compositions without intruding on them.

The ability of color to suggest mood often depends on creating an overall harmony of hues, and you can use pale color filters to achieve this – a brown filter to warm up overall tones or a blue one to give an impression of coolness. Diffusion and fog filters can evoke a dreamlike sense of the past, as in the picture opposite, below. And if you want to achieve a delicate pastel effect, you can try using a fog filter and a pale color filter in combination.

Graduated filters, with a colored half that fades gradually into a clear half, are usually chosen to add drama to landscape pictures. But these filters, too, can be used unobtrusively – as in the photograph below, in which the darkening of the sky at the upper left of the image creates the naturalistic impression of a dust cloud or heat haze over the rest of the picture. A filter holder, illustrated on the opposite page, enables you to move a graduated filter to cover the desired part of the scene. Lens focal length and aperture will affect how the boundary zone between colored and clear areas blends in. The longer the lens and the wider the aperture, the less perceptible the boundary line will be.

An isolated stand of trees *adds interest to a study of landscape colors. A blue graduated filter darkened the sky so that a dusty haze seems to hang over the cornfield. The photographer used a wide-angle lens at a narrow aperture to make the change in tone more apparent.*

Filter systems
The filter holder above takes up to three square filters, or two square filters and one circular filter. It is attached to the lens by an adapter ring, and different adapter rings are available to fit any lens size.

An earth excavator (left) makes an intriguing silhouette. The photographer used a No. 81EF brown filter to warm up the cool twilight tones and to unify the composition.

Lines of bare trees reflected in a still pond convey a mood of pastoral tranquility. The photographer used a fog filter to achieve the delicate hues and soft outlines reminiscent of early photographs, and set a small aperture to suggest mist fading into the distance.

Starburst and diffraction filters

Dazzling flashes of sunlight on a pool of water enchant the eye, but on film they often look disappointing. A starburst or diffraction filter can restore the brilliance of the reflected light, as in the picture below, and create an image that more closely resembles what you remember seeing at the moment you released the shutter.

Tiny grooves on starburst filters and diffraction filters, as shown at the top of the opposite page, spread light from the bright highlights into the darker areas of a picture. Thus, both types of filters work best with scenes that show very bright subjects on a dim background. At night, for example, they enhance the twinkling brightness of street lights seen against the dark sky. A diffraction filter has an additional effect: it splits light into component colors, surrounding each bright highlight with rainbow-colored streaks or with halos, as at bottom right on the opposite page.

The effects of starburst and diffraction filters depend on the focal length of your lens and on the aperture you are using. However, the image in the camera's viewfinder does not always show precisely how the picture will appear, even if you stop the lens down to the working aperture. Take pictures at several different apertures, and choose the best effect after you have processed the film. Avoid using either a starburst or diffraction filter when a subject has a lot of fine detail; because both filters cause some diffusion, the picture may look blurred.

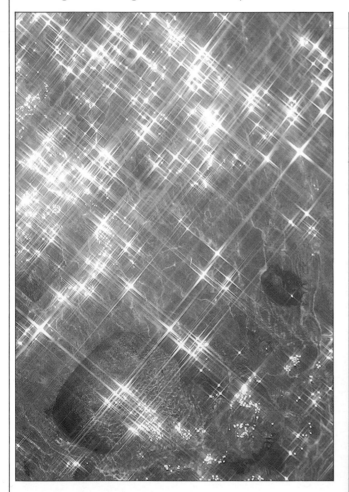

A rock pool glitters in the sun. *By attaching a starburst filter to the lens, the photographer turned each reflection into a four-point star. He also oriented the spikes of each star diagonally across the frame by rotating the filter an eighth of a turn.*

Choosing a filter

The pattern and spacing of lines etched on a starburst filter, illustrated below at right, control the appearance of the spokes that radiate from each light source. In the picture sequence, parallel lines create two-point starbursts (1), whereas lines at 90° and 22° produce four and 16 spikes on each highlight (2 and 3). On diffraction filters, the lines are too small and closely spaced to see; you can observe their effect only by holding the filter to the light.

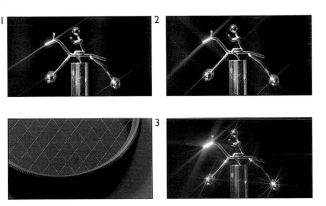

A misty window (below), when seen through a halo diffraction filter, spins rings of color around the reflected afternoon sun. By drawing a black curtain behind the window, the photographer ensured that the spectrum of colors appeared rich and saturated.

Spears of color (left), created by a diffraction filter, spill from the sun and its reflection in this upswept view of Fifth Avenue near St Patrick's Cathedral in New York City. Underexposure, and an additional magenta filter, helped make the rainbow streaks more prominent.

373

SPECIAL CONDITIONS

For the photographer inspired by challenge, unusual or extreme conditions provide one of the best means of getting remarkable and exciting images. Rain and snow, dawn and dusk, night lights and even harsh mid-day sunlight are among the conditions that can give you rewarding results as well as test your skill as a photographer. Equally challenging are the problems of using a camera underwater or in a theater.

Although the sheer difficulty or inconvenience involved may at times seem to be the chief obstacle, the challenge of most special conditions centers on problematic lighting. Today's sophisticated cameras can be relied upon to make proper exposures under normal conditions. But when light grows dim, creates sharp contrasts, or changes color, it is the photographer who must decide how to compensate.

Most of the techniques in this section require little more than paying close attention to choice of film, filter or exposure. But some activities, most notably underwater photography, require buying or renting special equipment. In the end, overcoming challenges to create memorable pictures is one of photography's most rewarding experiences.

Mountaineers and their tents stand out graphically against a mountain range. The photographer took advantage of a major picture-taking problem in snowy terrain – extreme contrast – to produce the dramatic silhouette.

Ice and snow

The pictures on these two pages show that freezing cold has its own visual drama and that the silent, still enclosed feeling of a midwinter's day can come through strongly in photographs. Although colors often vanish and the scene is reduced to monochromatic patterns of just three or four tones, this often helps to simplify landscapes that would otherwise be too complex. The frozen pond and woodland below gain coherence and impact in this way.

However, the subtle whites of frost or snow demand a delicate touch, especially in judging exposure. A mere half-stop may make the difference between an effective picture and an underexposed image that comes out gray, or an overexposed one that comes out bleached. On a day when sky and land merge in a unifying whiteness, underexposure is the more likely risk, because your meter will be fooled by the preponderance of light tones. Start by allowing one stop more than the camera's meter indicates for a frost-covered scene, and one and a half stops extra for snow. Then bracket in half-stops on either side of this setting.

You can create impressions of brittle coldness with details just as convincingly as with broader views, as the pictures on the opposite page show. Look for details that provide a strong contrast of white against black or in which frost creates interesting patterns and textures.

Hoar-frost (below) covers the trees and grass around a frozen pond. To be sure of conveying the icy cold of the morning, the photographer bracketed the exposures. One and a half stops more than the meter indicated gave the best results.

Sparkling icicles (above) hang in sheets from a rock face usually dripping with water. Because of the amount of deep shadow in the frame, the photographer did not need to allow extra exposure to record the snow's whiteness.

Frosty leaves (left) create subtle textures and colors. The photographer closed in with a 50mm standard lens at its close-focusing limit and gave a half-stop more than the camera's meter suggested.

393

Twilight and night

The brief period of twilight that follows dusk is an enchanting time to take pictures. Twilight photographs have all the special, calm beauty of night, yet there is still enough light in the sky at this time to make photography quite easy.

Following an afternoon of clear sky, twilight is a rich blue, sometimes tinged with the pink of sunset. For the deepest, richest colors, take a meter reading from the sky itself. However, this will record the foreground as a silhouette, and you will need to open up the lens by a stop or two if you want to retain a little detail in the land, as in the image of the tree on the opposite page. If you can include a lake, the sea or a broad river in the scene, the water's surface will help to spread the colors of the sky across the whole picture. This is the technique used to create the beautiful image shown below.

At night, the brightest moonlight is very much weaker than sunlight. Even with Kodacolor Gold 400 film, a moonlit landscape will probably need an exposure of about four seconds at f/2 unless there is a large expanse of reflective water or snow in the picture. Bracket your exposures, and use a tripod to avoid camera shake.

One way to cope with the dim conditions of night is to include the bright surface of the moon itself in the picture, as in the images on the opposite page at left and at bottom. Such photographs are most effective when the sky is still quite light in relation to the moon – shortly after sunset – and when the moon is at least half full. Check a local newspaper for the times of moonrise and sunset.

A still pond in winter reflects the subtle shades of twilight. Just after the sun had set, the light was still bright enough to permit an exposure of 1/8 at f/8 on ISO 64 film.

Llamas in Peru *(above)*
stand motionless during a
1/4-second exposure. A slower
shutter speed would have
made the sky brighter, but
would have introduced the
risk of the moon blurring
due to its motion.

Moonlit clouds *(right)*
dapple the night sky with
silver and black. By pointing
the camera at the moon, the
photographer was able to set
a shutter speed of 1/60 and
thus handhold the camera.

A rosy sky *(above) forms*
a colorful backdrop for a
leafy beech tree. To ensure
that the distant hills did
not appear as featureless
silhouettes, the photographer
gave one stop more exposure
than his light meter indicated
(ISO 400, 1/4 at f/4).

Tungsten lighting

Mixed lighting is characteristic of many nighttime photographs, particularly at dusk, when ebbing daylight may provide as much or more light than tungsten or other lights that have been switched on. While sometimes presenting tricky problems in terms of exposure or film choice, this kind of lighting also produces some of the most attractive color effects. This is particularly true when one source of light predominates in the picture while another provides contrasting color accents.

The basic rule for mixing tungsten and daylight is to decide which light source dominates, and choose a film balanced to that. Outdoors, just before nightfall, the main illumination comes usually from the daylight. On daylight film, the tungsten lights will appear orange, as in the pictures below. When there is less daylight than tungsten light, you could decide to use a conversion filter – or a slide film balanced for tungsten light – in order to show tungsten-lit colors more accurately.

The choice between daylight and tungsten light

film becomes more crucial for pictures of interiors in which you need to use a mixture of daylight and room lighting. If daylight from windows predominates, and particularly if the windows appear in the picture, there is no need to change from daylight film. The warm orange of tungsten room lights will add to the atmosphere, as in the interior scene on the opposite page.

In the early evening, or if the windows are small, the situation may be different, with the main light coming from the room lamps. To avoid everything turning orange, you should use a tungsten-light slide film – or a No. 80A blue conversion filter. Light from the windows will appear in the resulting picture as a shade of blue.

If you are undecided about whether daylight or tungsten dominates, always opt for daylight film. The warm glow of tungsten light exposed on this film is usually more acceptable than the cold blue of daylit subjects recorded on tungsten film, and looks closer to normal experience.

A streetlight glows in gathering dusk – daylight film records most of the scene in its true colors, but tints the lamp a warm orange (ISO 200 film: 1/30 at f/2).

The fish stall is lit by daylight, but the fish seller is lit by tungsten. On daylight film, his face looks orange (ISO 64 film: 1/60 at f/5.6).

A hotel lobby in Monte Carlo is lit by tungsten lamps, but daylight floods in through the glass doors. On daylight film, the tungsten-lit ceiling looks a rich orange, suiting the opulent decor. With tungsten light film or a color filter, the ceiling would have appeared in true colors, but the entrance would have looked a chilly blue. The photographer rightly chose to use daylight film unfiltered (ISO 200 film: 1/125 at f/4).

A Palm Springs street is lit bright by tungsten shop lights of varying strengths. Here, the use of tungsten film adds interest by deepening the dusk sky (ISO 25 film: 2 secs at f/5.6)

Stage lighting

Stage lighting during just one performance may range from an overall glow to a kaleidoscope of colors to a single spotlight. Judging exposures in rapidly changing or high-contrast lighting conditions requires skill and experience. Exposure meters may prove unreliable, even when the lighting is stable, but they are useful for indicating a setting to bracket around. Spotmetering gives the most accurate readings, but be sure to meter from a mid tone, such as a performer's face. You can save vital moments by using your camera in the automatic mode, and bracketing by adjusting the exposure-compensation dial. Cameras with an autobracketing function speed up the process and allow you to bracket exposures of fast moving action.

At a photocall, the lighting may be brighter than that for a public performance, and there is more time for careful metering. For the scene on the opposite page at left, the lighting was kept constant for photographers, making possible an accurate reading with a spot meter. However, photocalls often lack the atmosphere of a real performance.

A Buddhist monk *performs a religious ceremony on stage at an outdoor concert by Japanese percussionist Stomu Yamashta. From a central position in the audience, the photographer used tungsten-balanced ISO 160 film with a 50mm lens, relying upon his experience to judge the exposure at 1/30 at f/2 to achieve this golden, atmospheric picture.*

Spotlights beam down on a winged actor in a performance of Salome. *To ensure maximum detail in both shadows and highlights, the photographer took an exposure reading for the mid-tones. Because the overall lighting was relatively bright, he was able to freeze movement with a shutter speed of 1/250.*

The visual excitement of a rock concert or musical depends on rapid color changes and moving beams of light. These effects can look good even when frozen on film, but for less lavishly staged performances, the lighting may look dull. One solution is to use a starburst or diffraction filter, as in the picture below at right. Colored gels over stage lights affect color temperature, but it is unnecessary to attempt corrective filtration; even wildly unrealistic flesh tones seldom look disturbing on stage and can intensify the theatrical mood of an image.

A comedian entertains his audience at a nightclub (above). From his position on one side of the stage, the photographer used a 35mm lens, attaching a starburst filter to add interest to the upper area of the image. High-speed daylight-balanced film increased the feeling of warmth and intimacy common in such clubs.

Two Japanese dancers are frozen like marble statues under a spotlight at a photocall. The photographer took a spot meter reading and underexposed by one stop, preventing the bright highlights on the figures from burning out and emphasizing their sculptural quality by deepening the shadows.

405

Zooming challenges

Improved optical design has helped boost the reputation of zoom lenses, and professionals now regard them as capable of providing excellent image quality. Moreover, the range of zooms available has expanded in recent years: the familiar 80-200mm and 70-210mm models are now supplemented by wide-angle zooms (for example, 20-35mm), standard zooms (for example, 28-70mm as diagrammed opposite) and super-zooms (for example, 28-200mm or 50-350mm).

The complex construction of a zoom lens makes it heavier than any of the fixed-focal-length equivalents in the same range, even though it may be quite compact. However, if you treat a zoom lens as a convenient substitute for a multilens outfit, there is an overall saving in weight. With just two zoom lenses, you can cover an almost continuous range of settings from extreme wide-angle to medium telephoto, as shown by the photographs on these two pages. Furthermore, when the framing is critical and the viewpoint restricted, a zoom lens may enable you to obtain images that would be impossible with a fixed-focus lens. The wide range of framing options has special advantages for photographing moving subjects from a fixed camera position, for example in sports photography.

Using a zoom demands certain precautions and skills. With some "one-touch" manual focus zooms (that is, those with a single control ring to adjust the focal length and the focus), it is easy to shift the focus inadvertently while operating the zoom control. For critical focusing, you should focus with the lens at its longest focal length, pull back the control ring carefully and then make final adjustments to the focus. The number of glass elements in a zoom lens, often as many as 18, can cause flare when photographing into the sun. A lens hood will combat flare, but as an extra precaution you should preview the viewfinder image with the lens stopped down to its working aperture.

Another potential difficulty is reduced light-gathering power: the maximum aperture of a zoom is usually about one or two stops less than that of a fixed wide-angle or telephoto lens at the extreme end of its range. With the heavier, telephoto zooms, light loss may force you to set slower shutter speeds that result in a blurred image when the lens is hand-held. This problem of camera shake is particularly acute when you use such a lens at its longer focal-length settings. The best solution is to carry a tripod. Although adding to the weight of your outfit, this will give you wider scope for photography in dim light or for compositions that require a narrow aperture to provide sufficient depth of field.

80-200mm zoom, set at 80mm

35-70mm zoom, set at 55mm

80-200mm f/2.8 zoom lens

28-70mm f/3.5-4.5 zoom lens

80-200 zoom, set at 120mm

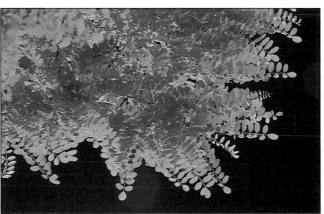

A two-zoom outfit

The 35-70mm wide-angle/ portrait zoom lens and the 80-200mm long-focus zoom lens shown above make a flexible outfit for travel, daily life or architectural photography. The precise range of focal lengths available will depend upon the make of your camera body.

28-70mm zoom, set at 35mm

Five nighttime views show the versatility of a two-zoom outfit. The photographer carried the two zoom lenses illustrated above, plus a tripod. He took these pictures within the space of three hours in London's West End, choosing a focal length appropriate to each subject. For example, the shortest focal length available to him was suitable for the dramatic skyscraper view at right, while the longest focal length made possible an abstract close-up from the same viewpoint (below).

80-200mm zoom, set at 200mm

Composing the still-life

Still-life is the one area of photography where composition is wholly in your hands. The exact position of every element in the image is your choice. Yet this total freedom can be inhibiting; you may not know where to start. Following some basic compositional guidelines need not limit your creativity and will help you build pleasing, unified images.

A still-life should be self-contained, whether it is a detailed study such as the flower on the opposite page, above, or an elaborately constructed scene such as the one below. Each ingredient should make a real contribution to the overall effect, with subsidiary elements supporting the main subject. This can be done in many ways: for example, by using lines to frame and lead into the subject, by

juxtaposing complementary or contrasting tones and shapes, or by echoing a pattern on a smaller or larger scale. The precisely balanced picture opposite, below, makes use of all these techniques.

A good way to learn about composition is to start with just two or three simple objects and practice moving them around to find the strongest arrangement. With the camera on a tripod, you can keep the view constant while you adjust the set and lighting. For more complex still-life arrangements, it is especially important to keep a strong focus of interest. Once the background and main subject are in place, add secondary elements one at a time, checking through the viewfinder to gauge the effect of each addition.

A country life theme links an array of objects. *The apparently haphazard arrangement was assembled in an elaborate studio set to produce a harmonious composition of natural tones and textures. Strong light from one side concentrates the eye on the main subject: the freshly cut foxgloves.*

Lily blooms (*right*)
stand out in strong relief
against a black background.
Centering the subject brought
out its symmetrical pattern,
while lighting on each side
and slightly behind revealed
its subtle textures and hues.

Speckled eggs (*below*)
provide the main interest
in an intriguing still-life.
Each element contributes to
the unity of the composition,
in which the echoing colors,
lines and textures lead the
eye easily around the image.

421

THE HOME DARKROOM

The marvelous advantage of home processing is that you have complete control over the results. You can make your images as small or large, light or dark as you wish. To begin with, you may decide to set up a darkroom just for black-and-white processing and printing. The basic procedures are relatively simple and will stand you in good stead if you later go on to making color pictures. However, with today's equipment and materials, there is no reason why you should not start with color processing if that is your main interest.

To start home processing you will not need a special room – just a work space that you can make completely dark. A bathroom, a kitchen or a dry basement laundry room makes a convenient temporary darkroom because there is running water to wash processed film and prints. But a large closet will do. Once film or color prints have been loaded into their lighttight processing containers, you can develop or wash them in another room. And black-and-white prints developed in the darkroom can be kept in a tray of water and later washed under running water.

To prevent damage from spills, keep trays and containers with chemicals away from the area where you make prints with the enlarger. And be sure the space is totally dark. Any chink of light will fog undeveloped film or paper. Consider making a removable window cover, using tightly fitted hardboard with black felt glued along the edges. Then cover that with a black curtain. A door may also need a curtain and a rolled-up mat to block the bottom crack.

A dry basement, with plenty of space for equipment, makes an ideal darkroom. Here, a black-and-white print is made on an enlarger. The red and yellow safelighting does not affect black-and-white printing paper yet provides a good level of light to work by.

425

Black-and-white darkroom equipment

A major piece of equipment used to print pictures is an enlarger, but you must also buy a number of smaller items. To develop film, you will need a developing tank and the reel that goes with it. Once you have wound your film onto the reel in darkness, and placed both inside the tank, you can turn on the lights and begin processing in normal room light.

To get consistent results, you must be able to measure three things accurately: time, temperature and volume. Any clock that has a sweep second hand will be precise enough to measure time, but to measure the other two variables you should buy a special photographic thermometer and at least two graduated cylinders.

To make prints, you can use the same thermometer and graduates as for processing film. You can also use the same clock, but more efficient is a timer that can be wired to the enlarger to automatically shut off the lamp after exposure. In addition you need three trays in which to develop and stabilize the paper prints and two pairs of tongs to transfer the chemical-soaked paper from one tray to the next. A safelight is also essential.

The enlarger magnifies your negative to the size of the print you choose to make, much as a movie projector throws an enlarged image onto a screen. Although an enlarger is not cheap, it is a one-time investment, and often you can use the same enlarger to print both black-and-white and color prints.

Finally, you will need an enlarging easel, often called a masking frame. This holds the photographic paper flat and positions it on the enlarger baseboard. Adjustable blades enable you to print pictures with borders of variable width.

Film developing equipment

Choose a developing tank and reel that match the size of the film you use. Some reels are adjustable, so that you can use them to develop both 35mm film and rollfilm. Buy two graduates, a large one for mixing chemicals and a small one for measuring concentrated solutions. A good choice of size is 32 and 8fl oz (1000 and 250ml). Many pieces of equipment you can find around the house. For example, although special film clips are available to hang up film while it dries, clothespins will do the job almost as well. A bottle opener is useful for opening 35mm film cassettes. However, household thermometers are not precise enough, so buy a darkroom thermometer. Rubber gloves should be worn whenever you handle undiluted chemicals.

Graduates

Storage bottles for chemicals

Rubber gloves

Developing tank

Darkroom thermometer

Protective envelope for negatives

Clock

Reel

Clothespins

Scissors

Bottle opener

Printing equipment

When buying printing equipment, always make sure that the easel and trays will accommodate the largest size of print you are likely to make. The enlarger itself should be capable of making a print 50 percent bigger than this, because you may want to enlarge just the central portion of a negative. A wide range of safelights is available from photo dealers. Be sure to use the appropriate filter recommended by the printing paper manufacturers.

Washing and drying prints

After processing, you must wash each print in running water for four or five minutes. An automatic tray siphon converts any print tray into an efficient print washer. If your darkroom does not have any running water, wash prints in a deep sink elsewhere. A length of hose attached to the faucet and a plastic pipe in the outlet will ensure a continuous flow of water, as shown in the diagram below.

You can dry most types of printing paper by laying the prints out flat on an absorbent surface, such as a clean towel or a blotter; by hanging the pictures on a line; or, more quickly, by using a hair dryer.

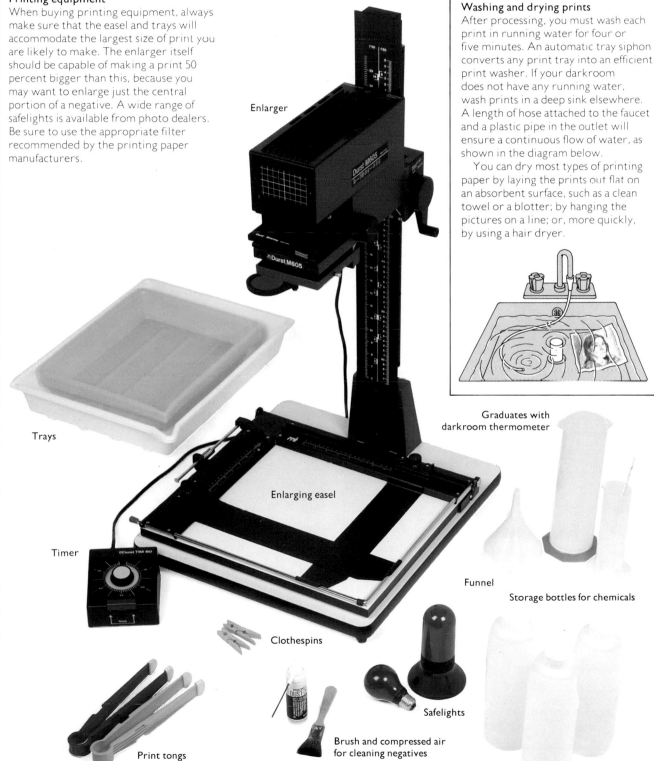

Enlarger

Trays

Enlarging easel

Timer

Graduates with darkroom thermometer

Funnel

Storage bottles for chemicals

Clothespins

Safelights

Print tongs

Brush and compressed air for cleaning negatives

Developing black-and-white film / 1

Because black-and-white film is highly sensitive to all the colors of light, you have to open the film and load it into the developing tank in complete darkness. If you are not sure that your darkroom is absolutely lighttight, you can use a changing bag, illustrated among the equipment at right. This is a special double-lined cloth bag that you can close and manipulate with the equipment inside, thus creating a totally dark environment for loading.

Developing tanks are designed to be lighttight so once the film is loaded and the lid of the tank is in place, you can continue processing in normal light. Two different types of tank are shown on the opposite page. Both are available in various sizes; the larger sizes are able to hold more than one reel of film for multiple developing. Each type of reel has advantages and disadvantages. The plastic edge-loading reel adjusts to fit any size film and is slightly easier for beginners to load. However, the reel must be absolutely dry before you load, or the film may stick or buckle instead of lying flat in the spiral grooves. The center-loading reel cannot be adjusted for different films, and the loading method may require a little practice. But once you have mastered the technique, the film will slide on smoothly even if the reel is not completely dry.

The techniques involved in loading film into a tank are quite straightforward. However, it is easy to make mistakes when you are working in the dark. A good idea is to practice the procedures a few times with the lights on, using an old roll of film. When you can handle each stage successfully with your eyes shut, have a final run-through in the dark. Following a few general rules will minimize the chance of error. Always begin with a tidy, well-organized working area. Put away anything you will not be using, and keep all necessary equipment where you can locate it easily. Work with blunt-end scissors to avoid scratching the film, and close the blades after use. If you are loading in a changing bag, check that everything is inside the bag before you remove the film from its light-tight casing. With 120 roll film, make sure you can feel the difference between the film and its paper backing, so that you do not load the paper into the tank by mistake. With 35mm film, cut off the film leader and then make two short, diagonal cuts across the corners of the film strip. This makes loading the film easier.

When you load the film onto the reel, take your time and never try to force the film if there is resistance. If the film jams, do not panic. Carefully unwind and reload it, checking that the reel is dry and the edges of the film are square with the spiral grooves. Drop the reel in the tank and replace the lid before turning on the lights.

Equipment checklist
1 Developing tank
2 Reel
3 Changing bag
4 Bottle opener
5 Blunt-end scissors

Opening 120 film
Carefully tear the paper seal on the roll and separate the film from the paper backing. Peel away the tape that attaches the end of the film to the paper.

Opening 35mm film
With a bottle opener, pry off the cover at the end opposite to that from which the spool protrudes. Slide the film spool out of the cassette. Use scissors to square off the tapered film leader.

Preparing 35mm film
Using a pair of scissors, cut off the film leader and snip the corners off the film strip. This makes it easier to load the film onto the developing reel.

Tank with edge-loading reel

The components of an edge-loading tank are generally made of plastic. A light-tight container (1) holds one or more reels (2) with spiral grooves. The film is wound on from the outside toward the center, with two clips on the outer groove holding the leading edge of the film in position. Plastic edge-loading reels have adjustable halves to take different film sizes. A hollow black tube (3) fits inside the reel to funnel solutions into the tank. The tank lid (4) has a funnel that forms a light-tight channel to admit the liquid. When the lid is closed, the tank is completely lighttight. A cap (5) fits tightly onto the lid so that the tank can be turned upside down during processing.

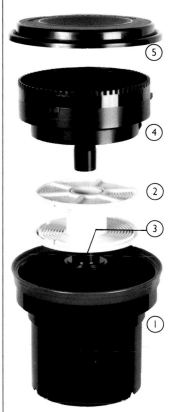

Tank with center-loading reel

The components of a center-loading tank are generally made of stainless steel. A container of variable size (1) holds one or more spiral reels (2) with a central core. A clip holds the end of the film, which is wound onto spiral grooves that start at the core and run to the outside. Center-loading reels are not adjustable, so you will need to buy a separate reel to fit every film size you use. The tank is closed with a light-tight lid (3), which has gaps around the inside so that processing liquids can be poured into the tank. A stainless steel or plastic cap (4) fits over the lid; when the cap is in position, the tank can be safely inverted during processing without liquids leaking out through the lid.

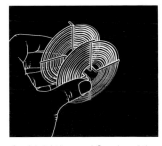

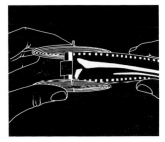

1 – Set an adjustable reel to the right width by sharply twisting the halves until they click into position.

2 – Line up the slots on the outer rim and, holding the film by the edges, feed the end into the outer groove.

1 – Hold the reel firmly with the sides vertical. Rotate the reel until the blunt ends of the spiral are at the top.

2 – Bow the film slightly between thumb and forefinger and insert the end into the clip in the core of the reel.

3 – Rotate the two halves of the reel alternately and in opposite directions, keeping the film smooth and straight.

4 – Cut the end off the roll or magazine to leave a neat edge when the whole film has been wound into the grooves.

3 – Continue to bow the film as you rotate the reel away from it. Gently slide the film on; do not scrape the edges.

4 – When the film is wound on, cut it free. Check that each coil of film lies flat and that each groove is used.

429

Black-and-white printing/2

Just as film requires carefully judged exposure to produce a good negative, a sheet of printing paper requires just the right amount of light to produce a print that is neither too dark nor too pale.

To find out how much light the paper needs for the image you are projecting, you must make a test print. This is a strip of paper cut from a full sheet, on which you print a section of the negative. But instead of giving the whole strip the same exposure, you follow the procedure shown on the opposite page (steps 1 to 8) to make a series of exposures of increasing duration. After processing the test strip, you can judge which time produced the best results, and expose the full print accordingly (steps 9 to 12). The box below will help you to work out how much exposure each section of the test should receive.

For the test to provide a reliable guide to exposure, you must process the strip – and the print that follows – with a little more care than you take when processing a contact print. When you mix the developer, use water at 68°F (20°C), or warmer if the developer concentrate is cold. This way the temperature of the developer should be right for developing both the test and the print. Do not worry if the developer temperature falls one degree during your printing session – such a small change is unimportant. In a cold room, you can prevent excessive cooling by standing the tray of developer in a larger tray of warm water. The temperatures of the stop and fixer baths are less crucial than that of the developer.

Processing time is significant, too. With resin-coated paper (the most common type of photographic paper), your test and print will need about one and a half minutes in the developer. Make sure that you use exactly the same developing time for the print as you did for the test, or your result may be unsatisfactory. If the test strip appears to be darkening much too rapidly in the developer, resist the temptation to lift the paper from the tray prematurely. A half-developed test strip has about as much value for exposure estimates as no test at all.

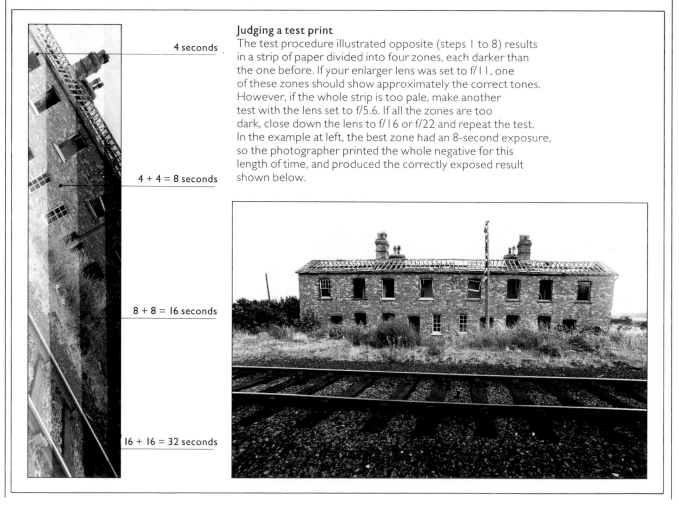

4 seconds

4 + 4 = 8 seconds

8 + 8 = 16 seconds

16 + 16 = 32 seconds

Judging a test print
The test procedure illustrated opposite (steps 1 to 8) results in a strip of paper divided into four zones, each darker than the one before. If your enlarger lens was set to f/11, one of these zones should show approximately the correct tones. However, if the whole strip is too pale, make another test with the lens set to f/5.6. If all the zones are too dark, close down the lens to f/16 or f/22 and repeat the test. In the example at left, the best zone had an 8-second exposure, so the photographer printed the whole negative for this length of time, and produced the correctly exposed result shown below.

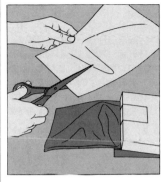

1 – Cut a strip of printing paper about two inches (5cm) wide. Put the remainder back in the black envelope, and close the box.

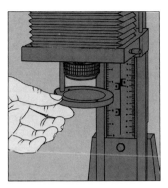

2 – Swing the red filter over the lens to prevent the blue-light-sensitive paper from being exposed. Turn on the enlarger lamp.

3 – Position the paper in an area of the image that shows both dark and light tones. Turn off the lamp and swing the red filter aside.

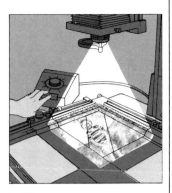

4 – Turn on the enlarger lamp to expose the whole test strip. After four seconds have elapsed, switch the lamp off again.

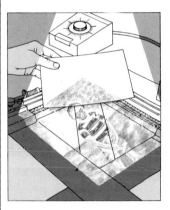

5 – Cover a quarter of the paper with a piece of cardboard and expose the rest of the test print – again, for a four-second period.

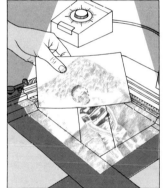

6 – Move the cardboard so that it covers half the strip of paper, and make another exposure, this time for eight seconds.

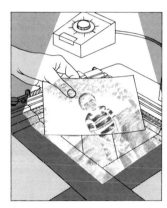

7 – Move the cardboard again, so that it now covers three-quarters of the paper. Expose the remaining quarter for 16 seconds.

8 – Process the test print and then pick the zone in the strip that shows the best tones. Note the exposure time given for that zone.

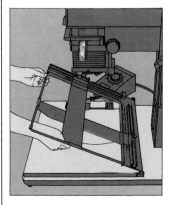

9 – Place a full sheet of paper on the easel, swing the red filter across, and turn on the enlarger to make a final check on composition.

10 – Check that the lens is set to the correct aperture, then switch off the enlarger lamp and swing the red filter out of the light path.

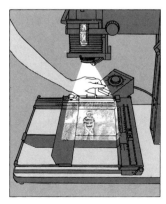

11 – Switch on the enlarger to expose the paper. After the time indicated by the test print has elapsed, switch off the enlarger lamp.

12 – Process the print as before. Make sure that the print stays in the developer for the same time as the exposure test.

437

Making a final print

Your color test will show four different zones, one of which should have more or less correct color balance. On the back of the sheet, jot down the filtration that you used for each quadrant. One or two of the four zones may be lighter than the others. This is quite normal. The cause is the absorption of light by the enlarger's color filters, and when you make the finished print you must make an exposure adjustment, as explained at right, to compensate for the absorbed light.

If none of your tests has perfect color, you will have to make a further filter change. Usually, the required change in the filter pack will be quite small, but this process of fine-tuning the color can actually be more difficult than the earlier correction of heavy color casts. This is because subtle color casts are hard to identify; it is easy to see that there is something wrong, but the remedy is not quite so clear. The ring-around chart on the opposite page will help you to identify an elusive color cast. You may also find it useful to look at the color test through gelatin color-printing filters. Remember that the color of filter that makes the test look right is the one you should remove from the filter pack before making the final print.

Filter factors						
Filter value	05	10	20	30	40	50
Yellow	1.0	1.1	1.1	1.1	1.1	1.1
Magenta	1.2	1.3	1.5	1.7	1.9	2.3

When you change filtration, you increase or decrease the amount of light that reaches the negative and the paper; to maintain the print density, you must adjust the exposure time to compensate. If you *add* an extra filter, you should *multiply* the exposure time by the corresponding factor shown in the chart above. And remember to *divide* by the same factor when you *remove* filters from the enlarger.

A color test (below left) shows how changes in filtration affect the print color. The photographer made the final print (below) at the filtration used for the bottom left quadrant but gave extra exposure to compensate for the added filters, as explained above.

Filter ring-around

If you cannot identify the color cast in your print, try to match it with the color bias of one of the twelve patches on this chart, then note the corrective filtration that you must apply to make a good color print. You may even wish to make your own ring-around instead of using a printed one. Do this by systematically changing filtration between prints, but remember to adjust exposure, as explained in the box on the opposite page.

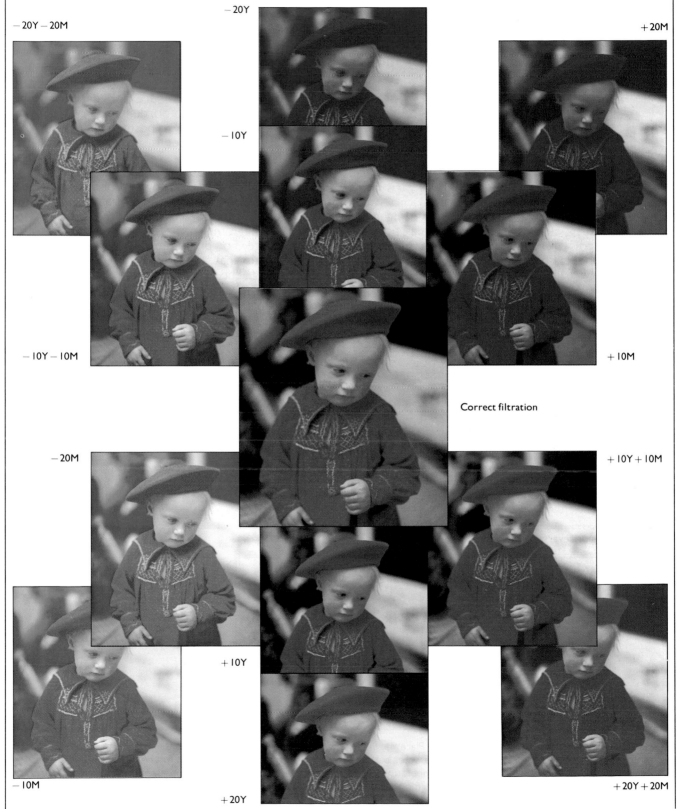

−20Y −20M

−20Y

+20M

−10Y

−10Y −10M

+10M

Correct filtration

−20M

+10Y +10M

−10M

+10Y

+20Y

+20Y +20M

PRESENTING YOUR PICTURES

Photographs are meant to be seen, and the lasting pleasure of photography comes after the pictures are taken and processed and you can browse through your prints and slides. Selecting, arranging and presenting your pictures are as much parts of the creative process of photography as composing and lighting, and deserve as much care.

The following pages explain how to put your pictures in order, and then how to show them to best effect – either in the form of an album or as a slide show, perhaps using a soundtrack with commentary. Whatever the mode of presentation, you should try to arrange your pictures in some logical order suggested by the pictures themselves. You might arrange them consecutively in a chronological or story-telling sequence. Or you might link together images that share themes or motifs. Keeping this in mind when you are taking pictures can pay off nicely when you show them.

When you begin to sort through your pictures, make sure you can study the images together. Allow plenty of space to spread out your prints or, as shown here, use a light box for viewing slides. And no matter how well you have planned your shots, keep an open mind – you may find that an unexpected theme suddenly occurs to you.

A photographer *examines* *her slides on a light box and* *lists their details in a* *notebook. Being organized* *is as much a key to producing* *an interesting slide show* *as creativity.*

K. Taconis/Magnum. **245** Bullaty/Lomeo/Image Bank. **246** Wisniewski/Zefa. **247** Morris Guariglia. **248-249** E. Sattler/Explorer. **249** Bullaty/Lomeo/Image Bank.

The Traveling Camera
250-251 John Hedgecoe. **254** l Dr. A. Berger/Daily Telegraph Colour Library, r Pat Morris/Daily Telegraph Colour Library. **255** l D. Williams/Daily Telegraph Colour Library, r R. G. Williamson/Daily Telegraph Colour Library. **256** t Anne Conway, b Michael Freeman. **257** l r Alain Choisnet/Image Bank. **258** l Robin Laurance. **259** l Michael Freeman, r John Garrett. **260** l Jake Rajs/Image Bank, r Vautier/de Nanxe. **261** t Ian Murphy, bl Richard Haughton, br Andrew De Lory. **262** l Bullarty/Lomeo/Image Bank, r Anne Conway. **263** t b Michelle Garrett. **264-265** All Adam Woolfit/Susan Griggs Agency. **266-267** All Harry Gruyaert/Magnum. **268-271** All Michael Freeman.

The Natural Landscape
272-273 Bill Brooks/Daily Telegraph Colour Library. **274** Reflejo/Susan Griggs Agency. **275** t Dennis Stock/Magnum, b Erich Hartmann/Magnum. **276-277** John Hedgecoe. **277** Paul Keel. **278** t John Sims, b Harald Sund/Image Bank. **279** Andrew De Lory. **280** John Cleare. **280-281** John Cleare. **281** John Garrett. **282** t b Michael Freeman. **283** t Dennis Stock/Magnum, b Michael Freeman. **284** t Adam Woolfit/Susan Griggs Agency, b Richard Dudley-Smith. **285** l Dennis Stock Magnum, r John Hedgecoe. **286-287** Jürg Blatter. **287** l Linda Burgess, b John Sims. **288** t R. Ian Lloyd/Susan Griggs Agency, b Michael Freeman. **289** Uli Butz. **290** Robin Morrison. **290-291** M. Moisnard Explorer. **291** t Francois Gohier/Ardea, b Robin Morrison. **292** l Michael Freeman, r Ernst Haas/Magnum. **293** t Ernst Haas/Magnum, b Ian Berry/Magnum. **294** Marc Riboud/Magnum. **295** t Ake Lindau/Ardea, b Andrew De Lory.

Animals and Plants
296-297 Jean-Paul Ferraro/Ardea. **298** Jean Philippe Varin Jacana. **298-299** Farrell Grehan/Susan Griggs Agency. **299** L. Lee Rue III/Image Bank. **301** t Jeff Foote/Bruce Coleman Limited. **302-303** Ian Murphy. **303** t Jean-Paul Ferraro/Ardea, b Ira Block/Image Bank. **304-305** Dennis Stock/Magnum. **305** t Horst Munzig/Susan Griggs Agency, c Max Hess, b Lionel Isy-Schwart/Image Bank. **307** Hans Reinhard/Zefa. **308** t b Eric Hosking. **309** t Wisniewski/Zefa, b Michael Freeman. **310** t B. & C. Calhoun/Bruce Coleman Limited. **311** Hans Reinhard/Bruce Coleman Limited. **312** t Robert P. Carr/Bruce Coleman Limited, b Michael Freeman. **313** Robin Laurance. **314** t Reflejo/Susan Griggs Agency, b Jeffrey C. Stoll/Jacana. **315** t b Michael Freeman. **316** David Muench. **316-317** Dennis Stock/Magnum. **318** Jean Paul Ferraro/Ardea. **319** b Viard/Jacana.

EXTENDING YOUR RANGE
321 Julian Nieman/Susan Griggs Agency. **322** Heinz Kluetmeier/Sports Illustrated. **323** All-Sport. **324-325** Tony Duffy/All-Sport. **325** Steve Powell/All-Sport. **326-327** Leo Mason. **328** Trevor Wood Picture Library. **329** Al Satterwhite/Image Bank. **330** Nancy Brown/Image Bank. **331** Graeme Harris. **332** Andrew De Lory. **333** Chris Alan Wilton. **334-335** Ken Griffiths.

Catching the Action
336-337 Adam Woolfitt/Susan Griggs Agency. **338** t Leo Mason, b Michelle Garrett. **339** t Robin Laurance, b Jerry Young. **340** All Michael Freeman. **341** Tony Duffy/All-Sport. **342** Jerry Yulsman/Image Bank. **343** t Steve Powell/All-Sport, bl bc br Derek St. Romaine/© Reed International Books Limited. **344** l Don Morley/All-Sport, r Canon UK. **345** Janeart/Image Bank. **346** All-Sport. **346-347** Fred Mayer/Magnum. **347** bl Horst Munzig/Susan Griggs Agency, br Graeme Harris. **348** t Sepp Seitz/Susan Griggs Agency, b Alastair Black. **349** Ernst Hass/Magnum. **350** John Cleare. **351** t Steve Powell/All-Sport, b Burton McNeely/Image Bank. **352-353** Adam Woolfitt/Susan Griggs Agency. **353** t Horst Munzig/Susan Griggs Agency, b John Kelly/Image Bank. **354** Adam Woolfitt/Susan Griggs Agency. **354-355** John Garrett. **356** t Tony Duffy/All-Sport, b Alain Courtois/Kodak. **357** t Jean Rochaix/Kodak, b Alex Webb/Magnum.

Creating Special Effects
358-359 Andrew De Lory. **360** t Robin Laurance, b Anne Conway. **361** t Jerry Young, b Richard Platte. **362** John Freeman. **363** t Robin Bath, b Ceri Norman, **364-365** Richard Oliver/Xenon. **365** t Lawrence Lawry, b John Sims. **366** t Geoff Gove/Image Bank, b Andrew De Lory. **367** t Andrew De Lory, b Francisco Hidalgo/Image Bank. **368** John Sims. **369** t Robert Eames, b Ed Buziak. **370** Ed Buziak. **370-371** Tony Jones/Robert Harding Picture Library. **371** l Mitchell Funk/Image Bank, r Richard Haughton. **372** Robin Bath. **372-373** Tom Grill/Susan Griggs Agency. **374** l Andrew De Lory, r Clive Boursnel. **375** Photri/Robert Harding Picture Library. **376-377** Ed Buziak. **377** t John Hedgecoe, b Geoff Gove/Image Bank. **378** Richard Platt (Band of 2nd Battalion, The Queen's Regiment). **378-379** Tim Stephens. **379** Michael Freeman. **380** Nick Boyce. **380** Richard Haughton. **380-381** Timothy Woodcock. **381** t Ian McKinnell, b Timothy Woodcock. **382** t Anne Conway, b Julian Calder. **383** t Julian Calder, b Michael Freeman. **384** l Andrew De Lory, r Chris Alan Wilton. **385** John Hedgecoe. **386** l Richard Haughton, r Alastair Black. **387** Alastair Black.

Special Conditions
388-389 John Cleare/Mountain Camera. **390** Alain Choisnet/Image Bank. **391** tl Ian Bradshaw, tr Max Hess, b Michael Freeman. **393-393** John Sims. **393** l Lionel Isy-Schwart/Image Bank, r Horst Munzig/Susan Griggs Agency. **394** Trevor Wood Picture Library. **395** tl bl Michael Freeman, r Ch. Pinson/Explorer. **396** George Wright. **397** tl John Cleare, tr John Sims, b A. Nadeau/Explorer. **398** tl Robin Laurance, tc Graeme Harris, tr Andre Chastel/Kodak, b John Hedgecoe. **399** Pete Turner/Image Bank. **400** l Michelle Garrett, r John Garrett. **401** t John Garrett, b Niki Mareschal/Image Bank. **402** l Donald E. Carroll/Image Bank, r Ellis Herwig/Image Bank. **403** t Gerard Champlong/Image Bank, b Vautier/de Nanxe. **404** t b Richard Haughton. **405** l Darryl Williams/The Dance Library, r Robin Laurance. **406-407** All Vautier/de Nanxe. **408** t c b All Flip Schulke/Planet Earth Pictures. **408-409** Warren Williams/Planet Earth Pictures. **409** t b Flip Schulke/Planet Earth Pictures.

Studio Techniques
410-411 Charlie Stebbings. **412** l Michael Melford/Image Bank, r Graeme Harris. **413** t Hele Pask, b Trevor Wood Picture Library. **414** Tony Stone Associates. **415** t Gered Mankowitz/Rembrandt Bros. Photo Studios, b Pete Turner/Image Bank. **416** All Michael Freeman. **417** All Michael Freeman. **420-421** Charlie Stebbings. **421** t Bob Croxford, b Peter Williams. **422** Tony Skinner. **423** t Nels, b Tony Skinner.

The Home Darkroom
424-425 Laurie Lewis. **434** Richard Platt. **436** Nick Meers. **439** All Clive Boursnell. **456** Tim Stephens. **457** Tim Stephens.

Presenting Your Pictures
458-459 John Garrett. **460-461** All John Garrett. **464** All Michael Freeman. **465** tl cl bl tr cr br Michael Freeman, tc cc bc John Garrett. **466-467** John Garrett.

Additional commissioned photography by John Bellars, Paul Brierly, Michael Busselle, John Freeman, Michael Freeman, John Garrett, Laurie Lewis, John Miller, Nick Scott, Tim Stephens, Frank Thomas, Victor Watts, Timothy Woodcock.

Artists David Ashby, Kuo Kang Chen, Gordon Cramp, Brian Delf, Roy Flooks, Tony Graham, John Hutchinson, Alun Jones, Edwina Keene, Aziz Khan, Richard Lewis, Haywood Martin, Coral Mula, Sandra Pond, Andrew Popkiewicz, Jim Robins, Alan Suttie

Retouching Roy Flooks, Bryon Harvey, O'Connor/Dowse

Typesetting by Hourds Typographica Ltd, Stafford, England and Dorchester Typesetting Group Ltd, Dorchester, England